New Directions
P.O. Box 80611,
Lansing, MI 48906

Become
a Pen Pal

W9-AOB-277

The Pastor's Minute

A Daily Devotional For

People On The Go!

DAVE WILLIAMS

The Pastor's Minute

A Daily Devotional

For People On The Go!

by

DAVE WILLIAMS

The Pastor's Minute
A Daily Devotional For
People On The Go!

All rights reserved. No part of this publication may be reproduced, stored in a retrieval system, or transmitted in any form or by any means — electronic, mechanical, photocopy, recording, or any other — except for brief quotations in printed reviews, without prior permission of the publisher.

Unless otherwise noted, Scripture quotations are taken from the King James Version of the Bible.

Copyright © 2002 by David R. Williams

ISBN 0-938020-60-9

First Printing 2002

Published by

DECAPOLIS
PUBLISHING

Printed in the United States of America

BOOKS BY DAVE WILLIAMS

Contents

The Pastor's Minute

This book is dedicated
to all of our
viewers and listeners
around the world.

God's not looking for perfect people, but people with perfect hearts toward Him.

So... You're Not Perfect

God's Minute

...nevertheless, Asa's heart was perfect with the Lord all his days.

—1 Kings 15:14

...I have walked before thee in truth and with a perfect heart...

—2 Kings 20:3

The Pastor's Minute

I've known people who were afraid to come to church because they felt they weren't perfect enough.

Then I noticed something in God's Word. Father Abraham told a lie to save his own neck. King David lusted after a married woman. Even the Lord's disciples had imperfections: they had temper tantrums, prejudices, arguments, and on one occasion even denied Jesus.

I thought about this for a while and made a liberating discovery from the Bible. I found out this: God's not looking for perfect people, but people with perfect hearts toward Him. People just like you!

Three Levels Of Leadership

God's Minute

> But Jesus called them to him, and saith unto them, Ye know that they which are accounted to rule over the Gentiles exercise lordship over them; and their great ones exercise authority upon them. But so shall it not be among you: but whosoever will be great among you, shall be your minister: And whosoever of you will be the chiefest, shall be servant of all. For even the Son of man came not to be ministered unto, but to minister, and to give his life a ransom for many.
>
> —Mark 10:42-45

The Pastor's Minute

Have you ever thought much about leadership? Well, we're all leaders in some way or another. And I've found essentially three levels of leadership in all walks of life:

Level 1   Superficial Leadership: This is leadership in title or position only. Level 1 is surface leadership.

Level 2   Second Level Leadership: This is based on some knowledge and limited preparation, but usually just enough to get by. Level 2 is shallow leadership.

Level 3   Master Level Leadership: This is leadership based on the pattern of Jesus Himself. It's leadership that is servant-hearted and service-minded. It leads by love and by consent of the followers. It's the kind of leadership that brings true greatness to your life.

Today, live your life as a Master Level Leader and watch greatness come to you!

Quit Procrastinating

God's Minute

If you wait for perfect conditions, you will never get anything done.

—Ecclesiastes 11:4 (TLB)

Go away for now...and when I have a more convenient time, I'll call for you again.

—Acts 24:25 (TLB)

The Pastor's Minute

"Next week I'm going to look for a job." "When I have more time, I'll come to church." "I'll get organized tomorrow."

We've all heard, and even made, statements like these, but few of us realize the grave consequences of putting things off. Every time we delay a decision or put off an action that could be taken immediately, we're sowing the seeds of a deadly habit called procrastination.

Governor Felix faced an opportunity to make his peace with God before death called him into eternity. Instead, he told St. Paul, "I'll talk to you when it's more convenient." But he never found that more convenient time. The most important opportunity in his life, and through procrastination, he blew it.

What have you been putting off? A sales call, a kind word, time with your family? Remember, faith is always NOW!

Three C's To A Happy Marriage

God's Minute

> Husbands, love your wives, even as Christ also loved the church, and gave himself for it.
>
> —Ephesians 5:25

> You wives, submit yourselves to your husbands, for that is what the Lord has planned for you. And you husbands must be loving and kind to your wives and not bitter against them, nor harsh.
>
> —Colossians 3:18-19 (TLB)

The Pastor's Minute

Are you having fun in your marriage?

I read a shocking statistic recently that said only six percent of all people in marriages are happy and fulfilled. That's not good! Let me share three "C" words that will help keep your marriage fun.

#1 - Courtesy. Courtesy and good manners go a long way in a marriage relationship. Watch your table manners and, men, remember a woman likes to be treated like a lady ... with love and tenderness.

#2 - Communication. This means taking time to share with one another and being a good listener.

#3 - Commitment. Committed people are happy, mature people.

We're all different in certain ways, and it's fun to learn about each other. But a marriage is only fun when there's courtesy, communication, and commitment.

Plan For Stress Reduction

God's Minute

> For we would not, brethren, have you ignorant of our trouble which came to us in Asia, that we were pressed out of measure, above strength, insomuch that we despaired even of life: But we had the sentence of death in ourselves, that we should not trust in ourselves, but in God which raiseth the dead.
>
> —2 Corinthians 1:8-9

> I can't carry this nation by myself! The load is far too heavy! If you are going to treat me like this, please kill me right now; it will be a kindness! Let me out of this impossible situation!
>
> —Numbers 11:14-15 (TLB)

The Pastor's Minute

Have you ever been frustrated to the point where you felt like dying? If so, you're not alone. Millions face this kind of stress daily. Stress is a dangerous inner reaction to outer pressures.

Signs include:

1. Forgetfulness

2. Temper flare-ups

3. Inability to change harmful patterns

4. Desire for more and more sleep

5. Frequent depression and illness

6. Trouble keeping pace

7. Feeling like a failure

8. A sense of helplessness

9. Becoming negative and cynical

Paul in 1 Thessalonians, gave us a three-point stress reduction plan:

1. Get alone for a while

2. Learn to delegate more

3. Pray

If you are experiencing some of the signs listed above, remember to get alone with God, let others take some of the load, and be sure to spend time daily in prayer. You only have your frustration to lose! Give it a try.

Lonely In A Crowd

God's Minute

He is a father to the fatherless; he gives justice to the widows, for he is holy. He gives families to the lonely, and releases prisoners from jail, singing with joy! But for rebels there is famine and distress.

—Psalm 68: 5-6 (TLB)

And when you draw close to God, God will draw close to you.

—James 5:8 (TLB)

The Pastor's Minute

Have you ever felt lonely in the midst of a crowd? Have you felt like a castaway, isolated from the rest of the world?

If so, you face a universal pain called loneliness. It's one of the most devastating diseases in America today.

When we feel an emptiness inside, we search and search to find a release from this agony. But all human solutions seem to fail us.

The real road of escape is found in two simple steps:

1. Quit looking to people and things to fill the emptiness that only God can fill. Find a relationship with Jesus.

2. Get involved with other people. Build bridges instead of walls.

If you're in a prison of loneliness today, YOU hold the key to your freedom.

Boredom

God's Minute

> Come to me, all ye that labour and are heavy laden, and I will give you rest.
>
> —Matthew 11:28

> The Spirit and the bride say, 'Come.' Let each one who hears them say the same, 'Come.' Let the thirsty one come - anyone who wants to; let him come and drink the Water of Life without charge.
>
> —Revelation 22:17 (TLB)

The Pastor's Minute

Have you felt trapped in a monotonous routine with nothing to look forward to but more of the same? Are you caught in the cycle of the daily drag and wonder if there's more to life than the old 9-to-5 routine?

Well, King Solomon felt the same way. He even wrote this: "Life is empty and full of frustration." You see, Solomon lost sight of the real joy and purpose of life and sought to find fulfillment in pursuing THINGS...but these THINGS left him empty.

Finally, later in life, he realized his real problem. He had drifted from God. As long as a person's inner life is empty, he can never be satisfied.

That's why Jesus said, "If you're thirsty (that is, empty and bored), come unto Me." Now, there's a good idea for healing boredom. Get into the Bible and see what exciting things are promised and what God has in store for your life.

Life's Problems

God's Minute

> Dear brothers, is your life full of difficulties and temptations? Then be happy, for when the way is rough, your patience has a chance to grow. So let it grow, and don't try to squirm out of your problems. For when your patience is finally in full bloom, then you will be ready for anything, strong in character, full and complete.
>
> —James 1:2-4 (TLB)

> If you will humble yourselves under the mighty hand of God, in his good time he will lift you up. Let him have all your worries and cares for he is always thinking about you and watching everything that concerns you.
>
> —1 Peter 5:6-7 (TLB)

The Pastor's Minute

We all face challenges or problems from time to time. When we do, it seems we are tempted to handle these problems in ways that actually work against us. Ways like:

1. Withdrawing

2. Becoming sensitive and defensive

3. Developing an overbearing attitude, and becoming difficult to get along with

4. Or worse yet, we just quit

Here's a four-point plan — a better way to handle life's problems.

1. Ask yourself, "Am I really going in the right direction with my life?"

2. Ask yourself, "What are my strong points?" Then build on them.

3. "Steady plodding brings success." (Remember the turtle and the hare?)

And most important of all:

4. Cast your cares on Jesus - because He *really does* care for you!

Entanglements

God's Minute

> He that loveth not knoweth not God; for God is love.
>
> —1 John 4:8

> For the wages of sin is death; but the gift of God is eternal life through Jesus Christ our Lord.
>
> —Romans 6:23

The Pastor's Minute

Have you ever found your life tangled up in such a mess you felt like choking? I think we've all experienced that.

The other day I heard a choking cry out in front of my house. I opened the door and there she was - my little white cockapoo - all tangled up in her chain. So I led her around the shrubs, around the pillar, and around the porch until she was untangled. Then I let her in the house. Was she ever happy! She jumped up on me and howled almost as if she was saying "Thank you."

Then I thought about others who might be tangled up in a mess today. There's a Bible verse that, in a word picture, says this: "Jesus came to untangle the messes of life."

It's true. If you're in a mess today, God will untangle it if you'll let Him.

Persistence

God's Minute

> And let us not get tired of doing what is right, for after a while we will reap a harvest of blessing if we don't get discouraged and give up.
>
> —Galatians 6:9 (TLB)

The Pastor's Minute

Sometimes we just feel like giving up - like throwing in the towel. Have you ever felt like that? If so, listen to this:

Two Frogs:

Two frogs fell into a can of cream,

Or so it has been told.

The sides of the can were shiny and steep;

The cream was deep and cold.

"Oh, what's the use," said Number One,

"It's plain no help's around!

Goodbye, my friend, goodbye sad world."

And weeping still, he drowned.

But Number Two of sterner stuff,

Dog-paddled in surprise

That as he licked his creamy lips

And blinked his creamy eyes.

"I'll swim at least a while," he thought

(Or so it has been said),

"It really wouldn't help the world

If one more frog were dead."

An hour or more he kicked and swam,

Not once did he stop to mutter.

Then hopped out by the island he'd made

Of fresh churned butter!

The point is: Don't quit. Hang in there - your miracle is on the way!

Distress

God's Minute

A merry heart doeth good like a medicine: but a broken spirit drieth the bones.

—Proverbs 17:22

So don't worry at all about having enough food and clothing. Why be like the heathen? For they take pride in all these things and are deeply concerned about them. But your heavenly Father already knows perfectly well that you need them, and he will give them to you if you give him first place in your life and live as he wants you to. So don't be anxious about tomorrow. God will take care of your tomorrow too. Live one day at a time.

—Matthew 6:31-34 (TLB)

The Pastor's Minute

Many people are distressed today. Their nerves are shattered over family, financial, or other problems.

Distress actually means to be tormented and worn down; feeling trapped. It's awful and can zap all your energy reserves, leaving you exhausted. But there's a way of escape. Read this carefully.

1. Believe what God says about you. He says you're a winner!

2. Take time daily to pray and clear the mental clutter.

3. Develop an unquenchable sense of humor. "A merry heart does good like a medicine."

4. Practice speaking positive faith words, regardless of how you feel.

5. Lean everything in your life on Jesus.

Do these things and you'll break the bands of distress and find real victory.

Lost Motivation

God's Minute

Jesus said unto him, If thou canst believe, all things are possible to him that believeth.

—Mark 9:23

But Jesus beheld them, and said unto them, With men, this is impossible; but with God all things are possible.

—Matthew 19:26

"And he said, The things which are impossible with men are possible with God."

—Luke 18:27

The Pastor's Minute

Are you bored with life? If so, maybe you've lost your motivation. Without motivation we become bored, confused, and just plain old hum-drum.

Motivation is that miracle "something" that propels us toward action and adventure. But what do you do if you've lost it?

1. Develop flexibility. That way you can bend without breaking.

2. Take life in bite sizes.

3. Take a vacation. Don't wait.

4. Evaluate your goals. Where do you want to be ten years from now?

5. Associate with "up" people. Their enthusiasm will rub off on you.

6. Don't try to prop yourself up with slogans and self-energy when God's unlimited power is available for you.

With these simple steps you can revive your motivation and revitalize your life. Pick one and give it a try today. Try another one tomorrow, and another one the next day. The next thing you know, you'll have all kinds of motivation!

Nervous Breakdown

God's Minute

Behold, the Lord thy God hath set the land before thee: go up and possess it, as the Lord God of thy fathers hath said unto thee; fear not, neither be discouraged.

—Deuteronomy 1:21

Fear ye not therefore, ye are of more value than many sparrows.

—Matthew 10:31

For God hath not given us the spirit of fear; but of power and of love and of a sound mind.

—2 Timothy 1:7

The Pastor's Minute

Are you a bundle of nerves? Do you feel "in a hurry" all over? If so, you may be suffering from the disease of this decade - nervousness.

It's true. The average life today is keyed to the breaking point, and that can be serious. Nervousness can destroy our relationships, disturb our zest for life, and wreck our peace of mind.

Here's a common sense remedy:

1. Plan your day and week with a workable plan. We often try to cram too much into our schedule.

2. Do one thing at a time. Nervous people usually scatter their efforts.

3. Learn to see the lighter side. I like to read "The Far Side Calendar" for a good laugh.

4. Practice the art of relaxing. Nobody can keep going at a tense pace indefinitely.

5. Live in God's presence. Only God knows how to tune the strings of your life to make it a beautiful melody.

Dream Stealer

God's Minute

> Be sober, be vigilant; because your adversary the devil, as a roaring lion, walketh about, seeking whom he may devour.
>
> —1 Peter 5:8

> Do not despise this small beginning, for the eyes of the Lord rejoice to see the work begin...
>
> —Zechariah 4:10 (TLB)

> Ask, and it shall be given you; seek, and ye shall find; knock, and it shall be opened unto you.
>
> —Matthew 7:7

The Pastor's Minute

There are dream stealers out there in the world today. Has someone told you "it's too late - you're too old" or "too young" or "too something" to make your dream come true? Well today, my friend, your dream is going to be revived.

Yes, there are dream stealers out there. They try to discourage you through fear, manipulation, or convincing speeches that say you ought to substitute your dream for something else.

But you're a winner, and here are some thoughts that will help you.

1. Know your dream. Write it down, and don't let anyone change it.

2. Recognize there are dream stealers. Be kind to them, but don't let them influence you.

3. Find God's promises for your success in the Bible.

4. Take inventory, and start NOW with what you have.

5. Remember, when you work with God, nothing shall be impossible unto you.

Don't let anyone steal your dream!

Bad News

God's Minute

And Jesus answered and said unto them, Take heed that no man deceive you. For many shall come in my name, saying, I am Christ; and shall deceive many. And ye shall hear of wars and rumors of wars: see that ye be not troubled: for all these things must come to pass but the end is not yet. For nation shall rise against nation, and kingdom against kingdom: and there shall be famines, and pestilences, and earthquakes, in divers places. All these are the beginning of sorrow. For as the lightening cometh out of the east, and shineth even unto the west; so shall also the coming of the Son of man be. But of that day and hour knoweth no man, not the angels of heaven, but my Father only. Watch therefore: for ye know not what hour your Lord doth come. Therefore be ye also ready: for in such an hour as ye think not the Son of man cometh.

—Matthew 24: 4-8, 27, 36, 42, 44

The Pastor's Minute

It seems like every time I pick up a newspaper or turn on the nightly newscast, it's BAD NEWS! It's disturbing!

• Earthquakes - over 200 a year now

• Governments falling apart

• Banking, political, and religious deceptions and scandals being revealed almost daily

• One-third of the earth's population is now starving

• Pestilences, new incurable diseases, killer bees, and new resistant strains of bacteria and viruses

• And I read that there are over 600 cult leaders - here, now - claiming to be Christ

What does it all mean? It makes you wonder if we're living in the day Jesus spoke of in Matthew 24. If so, that's Good News!

3 "Bones" To Success

God's Minute

> Where there is no vision, the people perish: but he that keepeth the law, happy is he.
>
> —Proverbs 29:18

> For verily I say unto you, That whosoever shall say unto this mountain, Be thou removed, and be thou cast into the sea; and shall not doubt in his heart, but shall believe that those things which he saith shall come to pass; he shall have whatsoever he saith.
>
> —Mark 11:23

> For as the body without the spirit is dead, so faith without works is dead also.
>
> —James 2:26

The Pastor's Minute

Do you want to be a success in life? Of course you do. And all it really takes is three bones. That's right...three bones!

WISHBONE...JAWBONE...BACKBONE

The wishbone is your imagination. God gave you an imagination to dream big dreams and desire great things for your life. Use it.

Then, there's the jawbone. That's speaking faith words. I call it "faith forecasting." Never underestimate the power of words. They become a force for good or evil in your life.

Finally, the backbone. Many use their wishbones, and there are always plenty of jawbones in gear, but the one who adds backbone - that's action - is the one who succeeds. A farmer who wants a crop has to plant the seed first. That's work.

WISHBONE, JAWBONE, and BACKBONE... Three keys to success!

Growing Older

God's Minute

They shall still bring forth fruit in old age; they shall be fat and flourishing.

—Psalm 92:14

For the length of days, and the long life, and peace, shall they add to thee.

—Proverbs 3:2

For they shall soon be cut down like the grass, and wither as the green herb.

—Psalm 37:2

The Pastor's Minute

I just realized something in the past couple of years - maybe you have too. I realized I'm getting older. I need glasses to find my glasses. Policemen are starting to look like kids.

Time changes us...and all the hair dye and face cream in the world can't stop the clock.

Mable asked Harry on their 50th wedding anniversary, "Harry, will you nibble on my ear like you did on our honeymoon?" When Harry got up and walked out of the room, Mable hollered, "Where you goin'?" "To the bathroom," Harry responded, "to get my teeth so I can nibble on your ear."

It's true: Time brings changes, but one thing never changes, and that's God's love for you. Why not set your love on Him? He's eternal and will help keep you young on the inside as you grow older on the outside.

Making Your Mark On Life

God's Minute

> You are the world's light - a city on a hill, glowing in the night for all to see. Don't hide your light! Let it shine for all; let your good deeds glow for all to see, so that they will praise your heavenly Father.

> —Matthew 5:14-16 (TLB)

> Verily, verily, I say unto you, He that believeth on me, the works that I do shall he do also; and greater works than these shall he do; because I go unto my Father.

> —John 14:12

> The steps of a good man are ordered by the Lord; and he delighteth in his way.

> —Psalm 37:23

The Pastor's Minute

Let me ask you a personal question. Are you making a mark on your generation? Are you leaving the world something to remember you by? Now there's a thought. How will people remember you when you leave this life?

Steven Greller, a Quaker who died in New Jersey in 1855, left us something to remember him by. Here's the short sermon he left us:

"I shall pass through this world but once. Any good I can do or any kindness that I can show any human being let me do it and not defer it. For I shall not pass this way again."

Why not decide today to make your mark on this generation and leave others something good to remember you by?

Enjoying Life

God's Minute

And also that every man should eat and drink,
and enjoy the good of all his labour, it *is* the gift
of God.

—Ecclesiastes 3:13

The Pastor's Minute

Are you enjoying life today? Saint Paul encourages us to trust in God who gives us richly all things to enjoy. That's right. God wants you to richly enjoy your life. And you can start by enjoying other people, especially those closest to you.

My dad died when I was fifteen, but I remember the joy I had when he spent time with us kids fishing, going for an ice cream cone, or just playing catch out in the back yard. I'll always remember those special times. Are you enjoying the people who really love you today?

Next, we experience the deepest kind of joy possible when we have a right relationship with the Creator. The psalmist wrote and told us the fullest joy possible is a close relationship with God.

So enjoy others, enjoy God, and you'll find yourself richly enjoying life.

Security

God's Minute

> There shall no evil befall thee, neither shall any plague come nigh thy dwelling. For he shall give his angels charge over thee, to keep thee in all thy ways. They shall bear thee up in *their* hands, lest thou dash thy foot against a stone.

> —Psalm 91:10-12

The Pastor's Minute

I don't know if you've noticed it or not, but doesn't it seem that the things we once trusted in are getting less and less secure? Jobs, for example. I talked with a lady the other day who worked sixteen years for a company and is now laid off indefinitely. It seems we slave for a beautiful home only to discover dangerous radons, whatever they are, coming up from the basement. We put bars on our windows to keep us safe from burglars, but when a fire strikes, we're trapped. I even read 179 contaminates have been found in our drinking water. And Social Security, well, we're told that when we 76 million baby boomers reach retirement, it will all be gone.

Honestly, I've come to believe the only true security that can be found today is found in God Himself. He's promised to protect us and to prosper us no matter what when we trust Him completely. Get to know this God, He will give you the ultimate in security.

The Basement Window

God's Minute

But remember this - if you give little, you will get little. A farmer who plants just a few seeds will get only a small crop, but if he plants much, he will reap much. Every one must make up his own mind as to how much he should give. Don't force anyone to give more than he really wants to, for cheerful givers are the ones God prizes. God is able to make it up to you by giving you everything you need and more, so that there will not only be enough for your needs, but plenty left over to give joyfully to others.

—2 Corinthians 9:6-8 (TLB)

For what is a man profited if he shall gain the whole world, and lose his own soul? Or what shall a man give in exchange for his soul?

—Matthew 16:26

The Pastor's Minute

Here's a good story: Now it came to pass that the stingy tightwad was dying. He had never let his wife buy a new dress. In fact, she had to practically beg for grocery money every week.

Now on his deathbed, he handed her a box. It was filled with money - probably tens of thousands of dollars - that he'd secretly stashed away over the years. "Harriet," he instructed her, "put this box by the attic window, and when I die, on my way to Heaven, I'm gonna pick it up and take it with me."

So she put it by the attic window. He died, but when she checked the box and the money was still there, she blurted out, "I knew it. I should have left it by the BASEMENT window!"

Now there are just too many morals in this story to amplify on any one of them. So let me just ask you this: When you die, will your soul pass by the attic window...or the basement window?

You can know for sure if you have a relationship with God and His Son, Jesus.

Ugly Cream

God's Minute

> Bear ye one another's burdens, and so fulfill the law of Christ.
>
> As we have therefore opportunity, let us do good unto all men, especially unto them who are of the household of faith.
>
> —Galatians 6:2, 10
>
> And let us consider one another to provoke unto love and to good works: Not forsaking the assembling of ourselves together, as the manner of some is; but exhorting one another: and so much the more as ye see the day approaching.
>
> —Hebrews 10:24-25

The Pastor's Minute

You've heard of beauty cream, but have you ever heard of ugly cream? Can you imagine applying ugly cream at night or in the morning?

Yet that's what selfishness does to us. It makes us ugly to others. It's like rubbing on ugly cream. But generosity and kindness make us beautiful to others no matter what we think we look like.

You've known people who are peppy, perky, kind, and giving. They seem so beautiful. And then you've known those who come around and talk about themselves constantly, complain about how they've been wronged, gripe, feel sorry for themselves, use people, pout, and act like they're some kind of martyr. Well, they might as well put ugly cream on every day because their self-centeredness makes them ugly to others. But you're not like that, are you?

I've learned that a relationship with God makes us more beautiful, no matter who we are. He takes out the ugly and puts in the beautiful by taking out the selfishness and putting in the kindness.

The Simple Life

God's Minute

Beloved, I wish above all things that thou mayest prosper and be in health, even as thy soul prospereth.

—3 John 2

Peace I leave with you, my peace I give unto you: not as the world giveth, give I unto you. Let not your heart be troubled, neither let it be afraid.

—John 14:27

But I fear, lest by any means, as the serpent beguiled Eve through his subtlety, so your minds should be corrupted from the simplicity that is in Christ.

—2 Corinthians 11:3

The Pastor's Minute

The next few pages are filled with five practical tips I'd like to share with you on how to be more productive and happy.

Many well-meaning people believe that God wants them sick, sorry, and broke. But nothing could be further from the truth. The Bible says that God wants us to prosper and be in good health - and it even gives us the guidelines for success and health.

Are you ready for Practical Tip Number One? Here it is:

KEEP YOUR LIFE SIMPLE

I cleaned out my office the other day and was shocked to discover a hodge-podge collection of confusion stored undisturbed for over a decade! Do you want a good rule for success and happiness? Keep your life simple. Avoid disorder. Discard the clutter. Clean out your closet. Trim down. Give the stuff to the Salvation Army or the Goodwill. They'll find a good use for it. If it's junk, throw it out!

Simplify and unclutter. It'll help you think better, feel better, and even do better.

Symptoms of Health

God's Minute

Don't be conceited, sure of your own wisdom. Instead trust and reverence the Lord, and turn your back on evil; when you do that, then you will be given renewed health and vitality.

—Proverbs 3:7, 8 (TLB)

Some people like to make cutting remarks, but the words of the wise soothe and heal.

—Proverbs 12:18 (TLB)

Kind words are like honey - enjoyable and healthful.

—Proverbs 1:24 (TLB)

The Pastor's Minute

Tip Number One on how to be more productive and happy is "Unclutter and keep your life simple." Here's Practical Tip Number Two:

LOOK FOR SYMPTOMS OF HEALTH NOT SICKNESS.

Have you ever noticed how people talk about sickness? "I think I'm catching a cold." "I think I'm coming down with the flu." "I think I'm getting arthritis." One fellow came into my office and showed me his vast pill collection for relieving his various problems. If he keeps it up, he'll need a cart before long.

But the Bible says, "The tongue of the wise is health." That means it's more profitable for you to look for and talk about health than it is to look for and talk about sickness. Can you imagine it? My phone rings and someone says, "Hey, Pastor Dave, I think I'm catching some health." Or, "Hey, Dave, I'm coming down with a healing."

If that ever happened, I think I'd...wait a minute, I'm not going to say that. The wise person speaks words of health!

Love Your Work

God's Minute

> Commit thy works unto the Lord, and thy thoughts shall be established.
>
> —Proverbs 16:3

> If they obey and serve him, they shall spend their days in prosperity, and their years in pleasures.
>
> —Job 36:11

> Not slothful in business; fervent in spirit; serving the Lord.
>
> —Romans 12:11

The Pastor's Minute

How can you be happy and productive? First, unclutter and simplify your life. Second, look for symptoms of health not sickness. Here's Practical Tip Number Three:

LEARN TO LOVE YOUR WORK.

In Genesis, we're told that God placed us here to work, be productive, and enjoy it.

I asked a bellboy at a hotel in St. Louis how he was doing. "I'll be doin' better when I get off work today." He didn't love his work.

Kemmons Wilson, on the other hand, founded the Holiday Inn franchise and became a multimillionaire. He loved his work so much, he only worked half days. He said it didn't matter which half he worked; the first 12 hours or the second. He loved his work and it paid off.

You can accomplish ten times more in 12 hours of uninterrupted work you love, than most people can accomplish in 60 hours of work they hate. If you can't change your job, then learn to love it. It'll pay off and you'll have blasts of energy you never knew about.

Diversions

God's Minute

> But they that wait upon the Lord shall renew their strength; they shall mount up with wings as eagles; they shall run, and not be weary; and they shall walk, and not faint.
>
> —Isaiah 40:31

> By faith he sojourned in the land of promise, as in a strange country, dwelling in tabernacles with Isaac and Jacob, the heirs with him of the same promise.
>
> —Hebrews 11:9

> And they departed into a desert place by ship privately.
>
> —Mark 6:32

The Pastor's Minute

Life becomes boring and monotonous when we find ourselves doing the same old things day in and day out. In fact, I made this mistake during the first five years of my ministry. We all know people who live, eat, and breathe their work. This can be a dangerous condition and causes people to become shiftless, idle, unhappy, and nonproductive in the long run.

Everybody needs a change of pace: a hobby, a sport, a vacation, a diversion — something to take your mind off the pressures of day-to-day work. Decide right now to do something different. Take a mini-vacation, go play golf, ride the roller coasters at Cedar Point, take a cruise, go shopping in Chicago. Do something different, and find yourself more productive and happy throughout the week.

If you don't go to church...try something different this Sunday. Go to church!

Love Never Fails

God's Minute

This is my commandment, That ye love one another as I have loved you. Greater love hath no man than this, that a man lay down his life for his friends. Ye are my friends, if ye do whatsoever I command you.

These things I command you, that ye love one another.

—John 15:12-14, 17

A new commandment I give unto you, That ye love one another; as I have loved you, that ye also love one another. By this shall all men know that ye are my disciples, if ye have love one to another.

—John 13:34, 35

The Pastor's Minute

So far we've talked about four keys:

1. Unclutter your life

2. Look for symptoms of health not sickness

3. Learn to love your work

4. Take on a diversion

The fifth tip for happiness and success is:

LOVE PEOPLE!

You've heard the Golden Rule? Well, it's still the best rule. "Do unto others as you would have them do unto you." Jesus Himself said it!

I saw an interesting study concerning the FBI's most wanted criminals. Not one of them who allegedly had committed these serious crimes had ever experienced any parental love. Love is a plan for success that's guaranteed never to fail. St. Paul said it: "LOVE NEVER FAILS."

All of creation is screaming out for love. Your wife, husband, children, neighbors, even your enemies are crying out for love. Genuine love can actually work miracles in their lives, and the benefit is you'll find love, happiness, and success for yourself.

Pressurized World

God's Minute

> For we would not, brethren, have you ignorant of our trouble which came to us in Asia that we were pressed out of measure, above strength, insomuch that we despaired even of life: But we had the sentence of death in ourselves, that we should not trust in ourselves but in God which raiseth the dead: Who delivered us from so great a death and doth deliver: in whom we trust that he will yet deliver us.
>
> —2 Corinthians 1:8-11

The Pastor's Minute

You and I live in a very pressurized world.

Twenty-five years ago, people were asking pastors, "How can I get to Heaven?" Today the question is, "How can I get through the day?"

We face pressures every day.

• The pressures of getting along with others

• The pressures to produce, perform, and turn a profit

• The pressures of school assignments, tests, and of being accepted

• Financial pressures

• Emotional pressures

• Pressures of misunderstandings

• Pressures from enemies; people who just don't like you and would like to darken your name

In this pressure cooker of life, we all need a resting place — a safe place where we can just let down and unwind.

Jesus promised such a place. He said, "Come unto me all ye who labor and are heavy laden (that means burdened down with pressures), and I will give you rest." There you have it. Now try it. It will work!

Do It Anyway!

God's Minute

> Preach the word; be instant in season, out of season; reprove, rebuke, exhort with all longsuffering and doctrine.
>
> But watch thou in all things, endure afflictions, do the work of an evangelist, make full proof of thy ministry.
>
> I have fought a good fight, I have finished my course, I have kept the faith.
>
> And the Lord shall deliver me from every evil work, and will preserve me unto his heavenly kingdom: to whom be glory for ever and ever. Amen.
>
> —2 Timothy 4:2, 5, 7, 18

The Pastor's Minute

You're a winner. I know that! I read something the other day I thought would interest you. It's called, DO IT ANYWAY. Here it is:

People can be unreasonable, illogical, and self-centered. Love them anyway.

If you do good, someone will accuse you of selfish motives. Do good anyway.

The biggest people with the biggest ideas are often shot down by the smallest people with the smallest minds. Think big anyway.

What you spent years building, someone may try to destroy overnight. Build anyway.

If you're successful, you'll win false friends and true enemies. Succeed anyway.

People who really need help may attack you if you help them. Help people anyway.

Give the world the best you've got, and you may get kicked in the teeth. Give the world the best you've got anyway!

ABCs Of Success And Happiness

God's Minute

Now faith is the substance of things hoped for, the evidence of things not seen,

But without faith it is impossible to please him: for he that cometh to God must believe that he is, and that he is a rewarder of them that diligently seek him.

—Hebrews 11:1, 6

Brethren, I count not myself to have apprehended: but this one thing I do, forgetting those things which are behind, and reaching forth unto those things which are before.

—Philippians 3:13

But seek ye first the kingdom of God, and his righteousness; and all these things shall be added unto you.

—Matthew 6:33

The Pastor's Minute

All of us want to be happy and successful, don't we? Of course, we do. And happiness and success are not merely a matter of talent, education, or skill. You and I both know plenty of uneducated, unskilled people who have achieved both happiness and success while others with phenomenal talent and education stand in the unemployment lines, even as we speak.

If talent and education alone cannot bring happiness and success, what can? Well, I sum it all up in what I call the ABCs of happiness and success.

A - Accept responsibility for your own life; don't blame others

B - Broaden your vision beyond the present

C - Challenge yourself to reach higher than ever before

D - Develop unswerving determination

E - Exercise faith

F - Forget the past

G - Give God first place in your life

Follow the ABCs and you'll discover overflowing success along with unquenchable happiness.

Kissing

God's Minute

Let him kiss me with the kisses of his mouth, for thy love is better than wine.

—Song of Solomon 1:2

So ought men to love their wives as their own bodies. He that loveth his wife loveth himself.

—Ephesians 5:28

The Pastor's Minute

Let's talk about marriage.

A young minister was conducting a wedding ceremony when suddenly his mind went blank. So he thought he would just quote a Scripture. After pronouncing the couple man and wife, the only thing that came to his mind was "Father, forgive them, for they know not what they do."

Actually, marriage is exciting and fun when the right ingredients are there.

And two of the right ingredients are appreciation and affection.

I read a study conducted by Dr. Arthur Sazbo which discovered that husbands who kiss their wives every morning live an average of five years longer than husbands who do not. Also, kissing husbands are involved in fewer auto accidents, are sick fifty percent less, and earn twenty to thirty percent more money.

So men, get busy! You don't need to be forgiven for marrying that little princess. You knew what you were doing. Just show her some affection and appreciation ... and give those lips a workout! We want you around for a long time.

Relationship Principles For High Achievers, Part One

God's Minute

A cheerful heart is good medicine...

—Proverbs 17:22 (NIV)

Pleasant words are a honeycomb, sweet to the soul and healing to the bones.

—Proverbs 16:24 (NIV)

The Pastor's Minute

No matter what your business is, you are in the people business. It's true! If people don't like you, they won't want to do business with you, promote you, or even listen to your opinions for that matter. So I'm going to share with you some of the important principles that will help you build relationships that will make a difference.

#1 - LOVE AND ACCEPT YOURSELF

Here's where it all begins. If you have a low self-image, you'll have people problems all your life. We can only rise to the level of our self-image; then we'll sabotage any further success in relationships. God put you right here, right now, for a reason. Love and accept yourself for who you are.

#2 - PUT ENERGY INTO BEING LIKABLE

If you're not pleasant, people will go out of their way to avoid you. Some folks just look like they have a major problem all the time. Try smiling often. A smile will always make you look and feel better. You will be surprised how many people will return the favor. It's an instant return on your investment.

Relationship Principles For High Achievers, Part Two

God's Minute

The memory of the just is blessed.

—Proverbs 10:7

The Pastor's Minute

We're continuing to discuss relationship principles for high achievers.

#1 - ACCEPT YOURSELF

#2 - BE LIKABLE

#3 - REMEMBER PEOPLE'S NAMES

Dale Carnegie once said, "A person's name is the sweetest sound they hear." So how do you make that happen? Well, when you meet someone new, repeat their name often throughout your conversation. Write it down so you can remember it.

#4 - SHOW GENUINE CONCERN FOR OTHERS

I understand that Nordstroms, a department store in California, does up to five times more business than any other store in its category. Yet their prices are higher. What is their secret? Quite simply, they care ... really care about their customers. In fact, they say, "The only difference between stores is the way they treat their customers."

#5 - FOCUS ON OTHER PEOPLE'S INTERESTS

You can make more friends in two months by becoming interested in other people than you can in two years by trying to get other people interested in you. People who have charisma are always "other-people focused." People who have no charisma are always thinking, "I hope I come off okay."

Next time you meet someone, think of ways to get interested in what interests them. When you're in a group, make it a point to make everyone you meet feel terrific about themselves. You'll be blessed by being a blessing to others.

Relationship Principles For High Achievers, Part Three

God's Minute

Love your neighbor as yourself.

—Mark 12:31 (NIV)

Whoever sows generously will also reap generously.

You will be made rich in every way so that you can be generous on every occasion and through us your generosity will result in thanksgiving to God.

—2 Corinthians 9:6, 11 (NIV)

The Pastor's Minute

#1 - ACCEPT YOURSELF

#2 - BE LIKABLE

#3 - REMEMBER PEOPLE'S NAMES

#4 - SHOW GENUINE CONCERN FOR OTHERS

#5 - FOCUS ON OTHER PEOPLE'S INTERESTS

#6 - ASK FOR HELP

Nothing makes a person feel more important than to do something for you. People need two things: to feel significant and to feel secure. Many of our young people don't feel they are important to anyone. Lack of solid family structure in children's lives has nearly destroyed any sense of real security. Don't hesitate to ask someone for their input or help. Make them feel important.

#7 - REMEMBER THE GOLDEN RULE

Jesus said, "Whatever you want others to do for you, do so for them." You want others to encourage you, so encourage others. You want others to appreciate you, then appreciate others. Do you want others to forgive you when you mess up? Then forgive others when they mess up. But always be genuine! No one wants to be lied to or given idle praise.

I'll warn you that sometimes it's not easy. But if you keep it up, you'll reap a harvest of such compassion and love you won't want to stop.

#8 EMBRACE A GENEROUS LIFESTYLE

This is the last principle I'd like to leave with you. Leave a good tip for the food server. Graciously give to charity without complaining or feeling like you deserve a purple heart for your sacrifice. God gives special favor to generous people.

These eight principles we've discussed will help keep you in the ranks of the high achievers in life. People will be glad you walked into their lives.

It's acceptable to remind others that our ears are not garbage cans!

The Sin Of Murmuring

God's Minute

Jesus therefore answered and said unto them, Murmur not among yourselves.

—John 6:43

Grudge not one against another, brethren, lest ye be condemned: behold, the judge standeth before the door.

—James 5:9

The Pastor's Minute

Have you ever known a chronic murmurer? Have you ever met someone who continually tears others apart with words?

Murmuring means to complain, grumble, to negatively affect the minds of others toward someone else by offering inaccurate information or ungrounded complaints. It's like a gang of workers holding secret meetings, debating among themselves, and stirring up trouble for the boss.

They hurt the company, they hurt productivity, they hurt profits, and they hurt themselves. The Bible says murmuring brings disease to the heart and can bring devastating and disastrous consequences.

When someone tries to contaminate you with their murmuring gossip or gripes, you can stop them with five questions:

1. What's your reason for telling me this?

2. Where did you get your information?

3. Have you gone directly to the person?

4. Have you checked out the facts?

5. May I quote you if I check this out?

When murmurers realize that you're not going to allow your ears to become their garbage cans, they'll stop. And you'll have a good day for a change.

Does God Work Miracles Today?

God's Minute

> But the manifestation of the Spirit is given to every man to profit withal. For to one is given by the Spirit the word of wisdom; to another the word of knowledge by the same Spirit;
>
> To another faith by the same Spirit; to another the gifts of healing by the same Spirit;
>
> To another the working of miracles; to another prophecy; to another discerning of spirits; to another *divers* kinds of tongues; to another the interpretation of tongues:
>
> But all these worketh that one and the selfsame Spirit, dividing to every man severally as he will.
>
> **—1 Corinthians 12:8-11**

The Pastor's Minute

Have you ever faced a situation where you needed a miracle from God? We've all read about miracles in the Bible. But the question is, "Will God still work these kinds of miracles today?" Well, let me tell you about an amazing lady named Ruby.

Ruby developed an incurable eye disease and slowly blindness overtook her life. The doctor had done all he could. She was discouraged and depressed, but she reached out to God, and visited Mount Hope Church one Sunday morning. She came up for prayer, and went home with her miracle; she could see! At first, I didn't believe it so I asked to have her doctor contact me. He did, and he even put it in writing. He told me what Ruby experienced was "nothing short of a miracle."

That was four years ago, and today Ruby still rejoices over being able to see. She's now a member of Mount Hope Church. We see her around here a lot and we call her "Bright Eyes," because of her bright, beautiful, miracle eyes.

To answer the question: Does God still give miracles today? Just ask Ruby. She'll tell you.

What Do You Want Out Of Life?

God's Minute

A man's heart deviseth his way: but the LORD directeth his steps.

— Proverbs 16:9

And the LORD answered me, and said, Write the vision, and make *it* plain upon tables, that he may run that readeth it.

—Habakkuk 2:2

The Pastor's Minute

Have you ever asked yourself the question, "What is it that I really want out of life?"

Lots of people speed through life hoping to arrive somewhere good but having no plan or strategy to do so. They just go through life hoping something good will happen. Like the captain of the 757 who came on the intercom and said, "Ladies and gentlemen, I have some bad news and some good news. First the bad news. We lost one engine. The other one looks like it's about to go. We also lost our navigation system. We have no idea where we're at. But the good news is we have a fifty-mile-an-hour tail wind and so wherever we're going, we're going to get there quicker."

Some people's lives are like that. They're moving fast but have no idea where. We're not like that, but if you know someone who is, there's a cure. It's simply this: write down where you want to be five years from now and what you want to achieve in life. Then ask God for Heaven-sent ideas on how to do it.

Five years from now, you'll look back and be amazed at how much progress you've made toward getting what you really want out of life.

Jim Abbot

God's Minute

> Death and life *are* in the power of the tongue: and they that love it shall eat the fruit thereof.
>
> —Proverbs 18:21

> Let no corrupt communication proceed out of your mouth, but that which is good to the use of edifying, that it may minister grace unto the hearers.
>
> —Ephesians 4:29

The Pastor's Minute

He grew up in Flint. Since 1989 he's amazed baseball fans everywhere, first as a major-league pitcher for the California Angels and then with the New York Yankees. A powerfully skilled pitcher, he even chalked up a no-hitter against the Cleveland Indians.

His name is Jim Abbot, and he was born without a right hand. What was it that drove Jim to succeed?

It was his parents who always blessed him with words of encouragement, never limiting his dreams; only encouraging him on. In fact, his father said in an interview that if all kids got the kind of affirmation Jim got, they'd all be top executives in the world.

Mom/Dad: Bless your children with kind words of encouragement every day.

Thanksgiving

God's Minute

Enter into his gates with thanksgiving, *and* into his courts with praise: be thankful unto him, *and* bless his name.

—Psalm 100:4

And let the peace of God rule in your hearts, to the which also ye are called in one body; and be ye thankful.

—Colossians 3:15

The Pastor's Minute

Do you know the power of thanksgiving? I mean being grateful rather than complaining?

Some time ago, a vibrant, smiling 58 year old lady visited Mount Hope Church and talked with me after the service. She told me she had been diagnosed with cancer. She was depressed and desperate when she attended an interdenominational service where I happened to be speaking on the Miracle of Thanksgiving. After that service, she told me she went home and started to thank the Lord for all the good things in her life. She said she actually started feeling better. About that time I saw it coming. She jumped up, smiled from ear to ear, hugged me, and blurted out, "Brother Dave, I went to my doctor, and the cancer is gone! Thank you for telling me about the Miracle of Thanksgiving."

And I thanked her for sharing that good report with me.

Find the good things in YOUR life to be thankful for. Write them down. Offer up a prayer of thanksgiving to the Lord and watch the miracles come your way.

Opening The Gate To Miracles

God's Minute

Offer unto God thanksgiving; and pay thy vows
unto the most High: And call upon me in the
day of trouble: I will deliver thee, and thou shalt
glorify me.

—Psalm 50:14-15

The Pastor's Minute

Do you know that thanksgiving does something
supernatural in you?

In the Hebrew language, we learn that thanksgiving - being grateful - actually opens the gate for
miracles. It brings some kind of supernatural grace
or favor into our lives. An interesting finding was
made by Jim Rohn, a man who's studied the lives of
successful men and women across America. He said

the number one key to happiness, achievement, and success is to FIRST be thankful. Amazing! We've all known gripers and complainers and criticizers. And it's true. They're not very happy people. They're in the majority.

But *you* can be in the minority and open the gate to miracles and favor in your life by being thankful. Success and happiness can be yours through thanksgiving.

Thankfulness

God's Minute

And it came to pass, as he went to Jerusalem, that he passed through the midst of Samaria and Galilee. And as he entered into a certain village, there met him ten men that were lepers, which stood afar off: And they lifted up *their* voices, and said, Jesus, Master, have mercy on us. And when he saw *them*, he said unto them, Go shew yourselves unto the priests. And it came to pass, that, as they went, they were cleansed. And one of them, when he saw that he was healed, turned back, and with a loud voice glorified God, And fell down on *his* face at his feet, giving him thanks: and he was a Samaritan. And Jesus answering said, Were there not ten cleansed? but where *are* the nine? There are not found that returned to give glory to God, save this stranger. And he said unto him, Arise, go thy way: thy faith hath made thee whole.

—Luke 17:11-19

The Pastor's Minute

Can you think of anything to be thankful for?

I saw an interview a few months ago with a Los Angeles Lifeguard - a real Baywatch hero. He said that since becoming a lifeguard he had rescued 223 people. And out of that 223, only three came back to thank him. Imagine that.

Jesus had a similar experience. He had just healed ten lepers, yet only one of them bothered to come back and say "thanks." That's incredible. Jesus said the one who took the time to say "thanks" received something the other nine did not. The other nine were healed, but the one who stopped to thank Jesus was made whole. That means that the others got rid of their leprosy but still bore the scars of what it had done to them. The Bible says the thankful man was made whole. His missing extremities, lost from leprosy, now returned.

It's true. Thankfulness leads to wholeness.

Reasons To Be Thankful

God's Minute

> And he commanded the multitude to sit down
> on the grass, and took the five loaves, and the
> two fishes, and looking up to heaven, he
> blessed, and brake, and gave the loaves to *his*
> disciples, and the disciples to the multitude. And
> they did all eat, and were filled: and they took
> up of the fragments that remained twelve bas-
> kets full.

—Matthew 14:19-20

The Pastor's Minute

Did you know that thankfulness can multiply
your goods?

Years ago I figured out how to hook two cassette
tape recorders together in order to duplicate tapes. I
made a copy of a tape for a friend of mine, and he
was so appreciative and grateful that I made him
another one. And then another. Even though it took

time, it was a joy because my friend appreciated it so much. He got quite a few tapes added to his library because of his grateful attitude.

One day the disciples were complaining of not having enough food to feed the people, when Jesus simply took what they had, gave thanks for it, and a miracle occurred. A few fish and a few loaves of bread multiplied supernaturally to feed 5,000 men. I think something miraculous happens when we're thankful for what we do have instead of complaining about what we don't have.

Try your own experiment today. See how this attitude of gratitude influences others in your life, and watch God multiply your blessings!

Blessing With Words

God's Minute

> Let no corrupt communication proceed out of your mouth, but that which is good to the use of edifying, that it may minister grace unto the hearers.
>
> —Ephesians 4:29

The Pastor's Minute

Did you know the power of life and death is in your tongue? Solomon said it centuries ago, and it's still true.

His name is Tom. He's 42 years old and he's a bitter, volatile man with an explosive temper, full of hostility, defensiveness, and furious energy. He spends every dime he makes on luxury artifacts to show the world he's somebody. Years ago, Tom heard repeatedly from his father these words: "Tom, you'll never amount to anything. You'll always be a bum.

You're just a bum." The words burned into little Tom's spirit like a branding iron into the flesh of a cow, short-circuiting his entire personality, contributing to his rage today. Tom was raised in a blessing-deficient home caused by a thoughtless father's verbal abuse.

Dad/Mom: Your words can help bring life and power to your kids. Make sure your words encourage instead of tearing down.

Concentration

God's Minute

For *in* six days the LORD made heaven and
earth, the sea, and all that in them *is...*

—Exodus 20:11

The Pastor's Minute

Why is it that some people seem to be able to accomplish five times more in half the time? How is it that some people seem to achieve more in one year than most people do in an entire lifetime? What is their secret? I think one of the important keys is concentration - almost a lost art.

Lee Braxton didn't even make it to junior high school, yet through concentration, he became a bank president, mayor of his city, and business executive owning several companies. At the age of 44, Lee retired and used the rest of his life to serve God through a well-known evangelistic ministry in America.

Lee, though uneducated, achieved more in a few short years than most folks do in their entire lives. His key: Concentration - Focus.

So much clamors for our attention today, distracting those who could be super achievers if they'd only learn to concentrate. Remember: Winners focus; Losers spray.

Do You Believe In Angels?

God's Minute

Be not forgetful to entertain strangers: for thereby some have entertained angels unawares.

— Hebrews 13:2

Are they not all ministering spirits, sent forth to minister for them who shall be heirs of salvation?

—Hebrews 1:14

The Pastor's Minute

Do you believe in angels? Johanna Day believes in angels.

She was not working full-time and had no health insurance, yet for weeks her physical system was out of order to the point where Johanna thought she was going to die. Crawling into her bedroom, she prayed to God that He would help her. She asked God if He was finished with her on earth. She was staring at the ceiling when suddenly the room filled with light. Standing at the foot of her bed was an angel speaking, "God is not finished with you yet."

Such a peace flooded Johanna's soul that she slept restfully for the first time in several days. In the morning she was well. Later, the doctor ordered liver tests which revealed that she had had a serious disease in the recent past which was now miraculously cured.

Are there angels in the world today? Ask Johanna.

False Prophets

God's Minute

> Beware of false prophets, which come to you in sheep's clothing, but inwardly they are ravening wolves.

> —Matthew 7:15

> Beloved, believe not every spirit, but try the spirits whether they are of God: because many false prophets are gone out into the world.

> —1 John 4:1

The Pastor's Minute

Has anyone ever warned you about false prophets? Jesus said, "Beware of false prophets who come in sheep's clothing but inwardly are hungry wolves."

Back in the 1950s, a huge outbreak of mercury poisoning struck hundreds of people near Minamata, Japan. Symptoms included:

1. a progressive weakening of the muscles

2. a gradual loss of vision

3. an impairment of brain functions

4. paralysis

5. coma

6. finally death

It was discovered that a factory had been dumping waste into the water. The fish were being affected, and the people were eating the fish. Contaminated food brought devastating consequences to those who ate it.

This is what happens spiritually when people feed on false teaching. Their faith weakens, they lose vision, soon spiritual paralysis sets in, and finally spiritual death occurs.

Make sure the people you listen to follow the values and teachings laid out in God's Word, the Bible. Don't become a victim of false prophets.

Children Are Treasures

God's Minute

Lo, children *are* an heritage of the LORD: *and*
the fruit of the womb *is his* reward. As arrows
are in the hand of a mighty man; so *are* children
of the youth. Happy *is* the man that hath his
quiver full of them: they shall not be ashamed...

— Psalms 127:3-5

The Pastor's Minute

The Bible says that children are a gift from God.
They can bring joy to a parent's heart, or they can
bring unbelievable pain. That's one of the reasons
it's so important to build the right kind of values into
children while they're still young.

It's not easy being a parent today. That's why we
built a state-of-the-art children's center at Mount
Hope Church. It is complete with full-time children's
pastors and trained workers.

It takes time to build the kind of values and principles in your children that will give them a special advantage in life and help them to be successful. The church can be a valuable part of that training. It can help your kids bring joy to your life.

Make a point of taking your children to church and watch the joy multiply in your home!

"One Minute, Williams, That's It!"

God's Minute

> Then he took her by the hand and called, "Get up, little girl!" And at that moment her life returned and she jumped up!
>
> —Luke 8:54-55 (TLB)

The Pastor's Minute

I have come to realize that a lot of things can happen in one minute.

At Mount Hope Church, it took Laurie, a veteran prostitute, less than 30 seconds to pray. She became a new person, never to return to the streets again.

With the aid of a friend, it took Ruby Jones, a blind lady, less than a minute to walk up to the altar. She walked away with her sight.

And what about Rick? He prayed a simple, short prayer concerning his future, and God gave him the job he dreamed about.

The little girl in our Bible reading for today was dead. She got her life back in one miraculous moment.

Come to think of it, one minute is plenty of time to make great changes in your life.

Why Are Some People Wealthy?

God's Minute

> For the love of money is the root of all evil: which while some coveted after, they have erred from the faith, and pierced themselves through with many sorrows.
>
> —1 Timothy 6:10

> Give, and it shall be given unto you; good measure, pressed down, and shaken together, and running over, shall men give into your bosom. For with the same measure that ye mete withal it shall be measured to you again.
>
> —Luke 6:38

The Pastor's Minute

Why are some people wealthy and some not?

Some say money is the root of all evil. But that's not what the Bible says. It teaches that the love of money is the root of all evil. You see, money is neutral. It can be used for good or for evil. It depends on the heart of the one using it.

I know a guy who never earned more than $12,000 a year in his whole life. Yet he retired a millionaire. How did he do it? Using biblical economics, he always gave ten percent and invested ten percent and lived on the rest. Following this simple plan made him a millionaire.

God's Word says, "Give and it shall be given to you in good measure." It also teaches that good people leave an inheritance to their grandchildren. The Plan: Give ten percent, invest ten percent. It's that simple.

Money

God's Minute

Whoever loves money never has money enough; whoever loves wealth is never satisfied with his income.

—Ecclesiastes 5:10 (NIV)

The Pastor's Minute

God said in 3 John, "Beloved, I wish above all things that you may prosper and be in health as your soul prospers." Prosperity is God's wish for you.

I've discovered the main reason why some never rise above financial mediocrity: They are not looking to God as the source of their supply.

In October of 1929, the stock market crashed leading America into the Great Depression. Out of desperation, many people committed suicide. They had looked to the stock market as their source of supply.

Indicators are pointing to another great financial melt-down within the next few years. Those who look to God as their Source will survive and thrive. Those who trust the wrong god will be in for a great let-down.

How about you? Are you trusting in the true God as your source?

Stinginess

God's Minute

> Will a man rob God? Yet ye have robbed me. But ye say, Wherein have we robbed thee? In tithes and offerings. Ye *are* cursed with a curse: for ye have robbed me, *even* this whole nation. Bring ye all the tithes into the storehouse, that there may be meat in mine house, and prove me now herewith, saith the LORD of hosts, if I will not open you the windows of heaven, and pour you out a blessing, that *there shall* not *be room* enough *to receive it.* And I will rebuke the devourer for your sakes, and he shall not destroy the fruits of your ground; neither shall your vine cast her fruit before the time in the field, saith the LORD of hosts. And all nations shall call you blessed.

—Malachi 3:8-12

The Pastor's Minute

Did you know that a stingy attitude is one of the key reasons why some fail to prosper in life?

Stinginess. That's right. Stinginess! We all know the guy who's so cheap he doesn't leave a tip for the waitress. And the fellow who constantly asserts that "All preachers want is your money." These folks reveal a stingy heart. God says this in Proverbs 10:4: "He will become poor who deals with a slack hand." In other words, penny-pinching, stingy misers will end up poor. In fact, as we read a moment ago in Malachi 3:8, we're told that a curse and all kinds of complications will come to the stingy person's life. But the generous person - who's good to his church, his favorite charity, and even his food server - will end up with the blessing of wealth. What a deal!

Friends

God's Minute

> Two are better than one, because they have a
> good return for their work: If one falls down,
> his friend can help him up. But pity the man
> who falls and has no one to help him up!
>
> —Ecclesiastes 4:10 (NIV)

The Pastor's Minute

Have you ever met someone who just doesn't
have any friends, or so they say?

We all want to have friends, but friendship doesn't
just happen I've learned. You have to be friendly
and be willing to be a friend in order to have real
friends.

A newcomer had just moved into the neighbor-
hood and decided to mow his lawn. But the
lawnmower wouldn't start, so he tinkered around

with it for awhile without any success. Just then his neighbor came over with a big chest of tools. The neighbor worked on the mower for a few minutes and varoom, it started right up. "Thanks a million," the newcomer said. "That's a fine set of tools you have there. Do you make anything special with them?" "Mostly friends," the neighbor replied.

How about you? Do you have a network of friends? You can. Just be friendly, remember the golden rule, and look for practical ways you can help others. It'll pay off in a big way, and you'll never be whining "I don't have any friends."

Teamwork

God's Minute

Two can accomplish more than twice as much
as one, for the results can be much better.

—Ecclesiastes 4:9

The Pastor's Minute

"That's not my job!" Have you ever heard that before?

The Bible says two people working as a team can accomplish up to five times more than two people working alone.

At a country fair here in the Midwest, a couple of farmers did an experiment with the winner and first runner-up in the horse pulling contest. Horse No. 1 - the winner - pulled 950 pounds. Horse No. 2 pulled 940 pounds. Then when teamed together, they pulled 210 pounds more than the total of what they could pull separately. Amazing! The power of teamwork.

Around the office or the plant, you can have a lot more fun with teamwork. Not only that, you make more friends and have better productivity. So when someone says, "That's not my job," determine in your heart to be the opposite. Not only do your job, but see how many others you can help with theirs. The results will be miraculous.

Do You Need A Miracle?

God's Minute

> ...for verily I say unto you, If ye have faith as a grain of mustard seed, ye shall say unto this mountain, Remove hence to yonder place; and it shall remove; and nothing shall be impossible unto you.
>
> —Matthew 17:20

> And Jesus looking upon them saith, With men *it is* impossible, but not with God: for with God all things are possible.
>
> —Mark 10:27

The Pastor's Minute

One day while I was reading the Bible, I discovered the ABCs of a Miracle. You can write for the full pamphlet, but here are the highlights if you need a miracle from God.

A. Assess your situation. This is the starting point for all miracles.

B. Believe in miracles. "All things are possible to Him that believeth," Jesus said.

C. Confess your own inability to meet the need.

D. Do what you can do. In other words, start with what you have.

E. Exhibit thankfulness before the miracle comes. Faith in action.

F. Forget the lies of the devil. He'll tell you there's no such thing as a miracle.

G. Give God something to multiply into a miracle. God multiplies what we give to Him.

If you need a miracle, remember the ABCs.

The Special Lady

God's Minute

Jesus saith unto her, Go, call thy husband, and come hither. The woman answered and said, I have no husband. Jesus said unto her, Thou hast well said, I have no husband: For thou hast had five husbands; and he whom thou now hast is not thy husband: in that saidst thou truly. The woman saith unto him, Sir, I perceive that thou art a prophet. Our fathers worshipped in this mountain; and ye say, that in Jerusalem is the place where men ought to worship. Jesus saith unto her, Woman, believe me, the hour cometh, when ye shall neither in this mountain, nor yet at Jerusalem, worship the Father. Ye worship ye know not what: we know what we worship: for salvation is of the Jews. But the hour cometh, and now is, when the true worshippers shall worship the Father in spirit and in truth: for the Father seeketh such to worship him. God *is* a Spirit: and they that worship him must worship *him* in spirit and in truth. The woman saith unto him, I know that Messiah cometh, which is called Christ: when he is come, he will tell us all things. Jesus saith unto her, I that speak unto thee am *he*.

— John 4:17-26

The Pastor's Minute

Let me tell you the story about a special lady in the Bible. She'd been misused, abused, and cast aside. She'd wandered from one dead-end relationship to another. No man had ever given her what she really hungered for, so she continued her desperate search down the long road of nowhere relationships. She knew the pain of five broken marriages. She felt special to no one. That is, until she met a man who called her something no man had ever called her before — special lady.

When He said that to her, she knew she'd never be the same again. The Man she met? It was Jesus. Write me, and I'll send you a pamphlet with the whole story.

Do you feel special today? Have you been wounded by the storms of life? Well, you're special to God, and like the special lady in our story, once you realize that, you'll never be the same again.

What's Really Important

God's Minute

> Whereas ye know not what *shall be* on the morrow. For what *is* your life? It is even a vapour, that appeareth for a little time, and then vanisheth away.
>
> —James 4:14

> To every *thing there is* a season, and a time to every purpose under the heaven: A time to be born, and a time to die.
>
> — Ecclesiastes 3:2

The Pastor's Minute

What is it that really matters when someone dies? As a pastor, I've conducted many funerals. Some are easier than others. But I'm always conscious of one thing during those tender moments, and that's this: What really matters at the time of death? It's certainly not achievement or success from this world's standpoint.

Saint James said, "Life is like a vapor, here and then gone." It's so temporary. I guess it doesn't matter how many flowers we have or how many people come to the funeral. We're still gone.

Solomon said, "There's a time to be born and a time to die." And the most important thing is not what day you were born or what day you died, but what you did between those two events.

So, I guess the most important question is this: Have I prepared for eternity by developing a relationship with Jesus, or have I lived only for this life? A good question to ponder.

Becoming More Popular

God's Minute

Wherefore, my beloved brethren, let every man be swift to hear, slow to speak, slow to wrath.

—James 1:19

Hear counsel, and receive instruction, that thou mayest be wise in thy latter end.

—Proverbs 19:20

The Pastor's Minute

How would you like to become more popular? Everyone wants to be better liked. Well, there's a little-known secret to becoming more popular I'd like to tell you about. It's simply this: Listen. That's right, listen. The Bible says, to "be slow to speak, quick to listen." Everywhere, people are crying out to be heard. "Listen to me. Listen to me. Listen to me, please."

Children are crying out for someone to listen to them. Listening says we care. People don't always need your canned advice. They need an ear, and listeners are more popular than talkers.

Do you want to become more popular and have more friends? Be a caring listener. Talkers are a dime a dozen.

To obtain the entire taped message on the Fine Art of Listening, call (517) 321-CARE. Be a great listener and let others know you care. You will never have a shortage of friends.

Handling An Attack

God's Minute

When they hurled their insults at him, he did not retaliate; when he suffered, he made no threats. Instead, he entrusted himself to him who judges justly.

—1 Peter 2:23 (NIV)

The Pastor's Minute

Have you ever been unfairly and falsely attacked? King David had been slandered by those who had called themselves friends, and this posed a threat to his good reputation. When he learned about the slander, he felt unspeakable distress and pounding at his heart. He felt drained. So how did he handle it? First, he put his trust in God. You can never prove something you haven't done. An appeal to man is fruitless, so David appealed to God.

Second, he recognized this was an attack of an enemy, not a friend. One who slanders and gossips is nobody's friend.

Third, he didn't compromise on his innocence. He didn't boast about being perfect, but he wouldn't agree with his accusers either.

Fourth, he remembered the law of the boomerang: he who digs a pit for someone else will fall in it himself.

When you face an accusation, like we all do from time to time, do what David did. You'll come out on top.

Facing Adversity

God's Minute

We are hard pressed on every side, but not
crushed; perplexed, but not in despair; perse-
cuted, but not abandoned; struck down, but not
destroyed.

—2 Corinthians 4:9 (NIV)

The Pastor's Minute

Have you had your share of bad things this year?
I know you've faced adversity; you've had setbacks
in life, reversals, perplexities, and struggles. Well,
how can you deal with them without losing your
mind? Five keys:

1. Understand that nobody is immune to adversity. Everybody, I mean everybody, faces it.

2. Know that adversity is necessary for healthy emotional and spiritual development. We hate it, but it's necessary.

3. Remember everything in life has phases. There's a slow-down phase and a set-back phase to everything. It doesn't mean that you're on the wrong track.

4. Learn the art of reversing it. Every hit was designed to propel you forward.

5. Ask God for inner strength to face the adversity. He'll give you more strength on the inside than the pressure is on the outside.

When You're "No. 2"

God's Minute

He must increase, but I *must* decrease.

—John 3:30

Let nothing be done through strife or vainglory;
but in lowliness of mind let each esteem other
better than themselves.

—Philippians 2:3

The Pastor's Minute

Have you ever met someone who's forever trying to impress people? I think we all like to impress people along life's journey because we all want to be recognized as someone special — someone of significance.

But what happens when someone a little smarter, a little more talented, a bit more attractive comes along? What happens when someone else takes your spotlight? Well, it happened to John the Baptist.

Crowds were thronging his ministry, and then one day out of the crowds came Jesus, the Son of God. What did John do when he became No. 2?

Well, he started by honoring Jesus and saying good things about Him. John knew that he didn't have anything to prove to anybody and neither do you. You're already special and important.

Think of this: Elisha was the No. 2 man, and he ended up doing twice as many miracles as his predecessor. Timothy was No. 2 and went on to build the biggest church in the First Century. It's okay to be No. 2.

How To Beat Fear

God's Minute

> Fight the good fight of faith, lay hold on eternal life, to which you were also called and have confessed the good confession in the presence of many witnesses.
>
> —1 Timothy 6:12 (NKJV)

> For God has not given us a spirit of fear, but of power and of love and of a sound mind.
>
> —2 Timothy 1:7 (NKJV)

The Pastor's Minute

Have you ever been worried or afraid? Do you think fear is just a state of mind or a mental attitude? Well, the Bible declares that fear is actually a spiritual force; it's the reverse of faith. Being a spiritual force, you cannot reason with fear. Fear short circuits your power, saps your energy, and produces tension so deep that your home actually becomes like a death cell.

Fear attracts the wrong things into your life. So, how do you combat this enemy called Fear? First, you must fight fear with faith. Faith comes by reading your Bible and hearing faith preachers. Second, fear and worry must be aggressively attacked as an enemy.

Saint Paul called this the good fight of faith. Say it: "Fear, Worry, you're through in my life! You'll have no dominion over me anymore!"

Finally, learn to be more carefree because Jesus promised to care for you Himself.

Power Over Demons

God's Minute

> Behold, I give you the authority to trample on serpents and scorpions, and over all the power of the enemy, and nothing shall by any means hurt you.
>
> —Luke 10:19 (NKJV)

The Pastor's Minute

I heard a story about a young preacher who learned about his power to cast out or excise demons. He walked up to a lady and commanded, "Oh, thou demon of gluttony, come out of this woman!" Just then he heard a voice say, "I will if you give me a cookie." Puzzled by that, he walked up to a gentleman and screamed, "Demon of procrastination, come out of this man!" Suddenly another voice responded, "I will, later, ha ha."

Those are cute stories, but did you know that Jesus promised His followers real power over the devil and his demons? He said that you could have power over all the power of the devil and nothing could by any means hurt you if you have a relationship with Jesus Christ.

Be sure to spend time in church this Sunday, where you'll learn how to have a close personal relationship with Jesus Christ. Use your authority over the devil, demons, and even the normal lassitude of life. Now *that's* power!

Are You Really Doing Great?

God's Minute

...casting all your care upon Him, for He cares for you.

—1 Peter 5:7 (NKJV)

And we know that all things work together for good to those who love God, to those who are the called according to *His* purpose.

—Romans 8:28 (NKJV)

The Pastor's Minute

An unusual thing happened to me a few weeks ago. I walked into a convenience store to buy a bottle of ginger ale when the clerk, John, asked me how I was doing. I told him, "Terrific." He then said, "I think you're lying to me." "No, really, I'm doing great," I assured him. Then he blurted out, "Yeah, well, a lot of people tell me they're doing great when on the inside they're dying."

What a statement from that clerk. I stopped for a Vernors but left with more than a soda. John's words kept ringing through my mind and my heart. I wonder how many times you've done that, said you're doing fine or great or terrific when really on the inside you're coming apart?

Maybe a bitter divorce, a sour business deal, or an investment that went bad. Maybe it's a doctor's report or just the weekly ups and downs of life. Everybody faces a feeling of dying on the inside at times, and it took a convenience store clerk to help me see that.

Do you need help getting through those inner battles of life? Your pastor or church care-worker is available to you. They will pray with you when things aren't going well, and rejoice with you when things are going great. Give them a call the next time you're asked how you are doing and the answer isn't "Terrific."

Who Can Take Away My Guilt?

God's Minute

> There *is* therefore now no condemnation to those who are in Christ Jesus, who do not walk according to the flesh, but according to the Spirit. For the law of the Spirit of life in Christ Jesus has made me free from the law of sin and death.
>
> —Romans 8:2 (NKJV)

The Pastor's Minute

Have you ever felt guilty about something? Guilt is a strange thing. It can cause you to see things that aren't even there and can cause people to do destructive things like over-drink and use drugs.

According to studies done at Harvard University and the University of Michigan, guilt can even make people more susceptible to certain diseases. So, how do you get rid of this destroying emotion called guilt? Well, you can take tranquilizers, but is that the real solution? You can try positive thinking, but you know as well as I that all good thoughts of the world won't take away the real stain of guilt from the human soul.

When Jesus died on the cross, He destroyed the power of both sin and guilt — the power of darkness that was bent on conquering our lives. Forgiveness provides the only genuine relief for guilt, and the cross is the only place you can discover that forgiveness.

Find forgiveness, comfort, and relief from the slavery of guilt this week in your home church.

The Man Who Has 15 Years Added To His Life

God's Minute

In those days Hezekiah was sick and near death. And Isaiah the prophet, the son of Amoz, went to him and said to him, "Thus says the LORD: 'Set your house in order, for you shall die, and not live.' " Then he turned his face toward the wall, and prayed to the LORD, saying, Remember now, O LORD, I pray, how I have walked before You in truth and with a loyal heart, and have done *what was* good in Your sight." And Hezekiah wept bitterly. And it happened, before Isaiah had gone out into the middle court, that the word of the LORD came to him, saying, Return and tell Hezekiah the leader of My people, 'Thus says the LORD, the God of David your father: "I have heard your prayer, I have seen your tears; surely I will heal you. On the third day you shall go up to the house of the LORD. And I will add to your days fifteen years. I will deliver you and this city from the hand of the king of Assyria; and I will defend this city for My own sake, and for the sake of My servant David." Then Isaiah said, "Take a lump of figs."

> So they took and laid *it* on the boil, and he recovered. And Hezekiah said to Isaiah, "What *is* the sign that the LORD will heal me, and that I shall go up to the house of the LORD the third day?" Then Isaiah said, "This is the sign to you from the LORD, that the LORD will do the thing which He has spoken: *shall* the shadow go forward ten degrees or go backward ten degrees?" And Hezekiah answered, "It is an easy thing for the shadow to go down ten degrees; no, but let the shadow go backward ten degrees." So Isaiah the prophet cried out to the LORD, and He brought the shadow ten degrees backward, by which it had gone down on the sundial of Ahaz.
>
> —2 Kings 20:2-11 (NKJV)

The Pastor's Minute

How would you like to live longer? Did you know that in the Bible there's a true story about a man who had 15 years added to his life? It's true. God told Hezekiah he was going to die, leaving his family and business behind. You can imagine how he must have felt when he received the news of his impending death much the same way people today feel when the doctor says there's nothing more medical science can do.

What do you do in a case like that? Well, Hezekiah did something you can do too. He turned his face to the wall, and he prayed unto the Lord.

First, he tried to get God to answer his prayer by complaining. Then he tried to get God to pity him. Next, he tried to get God to feel guilty for allowing this sickness to come upon him. But nothing worked until Hezekiah changed his prayer by first confessing his sins to God, then praising God for all the good things in his life.

Well, his praise moved him into the realm of faith, and soon revelation of healing came. The moment he was supposed to die was canceled. God gave him 15 more good years of life.

When you synchronize your prayer with God's will...your prayer will be answered.

Agony Of Unanswered Prayer

God's Minute

Ask, and it will be given to you; seek, and you will find; knock, and it will be opened to you. For everyone who asks receives, and he who seeks finds, and to him who knocks it will be opened.

— Matthew 7:7-8 (NKJV)

The Pastor's Minute

Have you ever struggled with the mystery of unanswered prayer? We've all faced the agony of what seems to be unanswered prayer. Someone once said, "There is no such thing as unanswered prayer; sometimes God says 'yes,' sometimes He says 'no,' and sometimes He says 'not yet.'"

Now this is not an original outline. I got it from Dr. James Biskirk, pastor of First United Methodist

Church in Tulsa, but I thought it would help you understand the enigma of unanswered prayer, so here goes.

When my request is wrong, God says, "No." If my timing is wrong, God says, "Slow." When my attitude is wrong, God says, "Grow." When my request, my timing, and my attitude are all right, God says, "Go."

You see, you're God's personal project. When you synchronize your prayer with God's will as it's revealed in His Word, the Bible, you'll hear the Lord say, "Let's go." And your prayer will be answered.

When Something's Gone Wrong

God's Minute

And Abraham journeyed from there to the South, and dwelt between Kadesh and Shur, and stayed in Gerar. Now Abraham said of Sarah his wife, "She *is* my sister." And Abimelech king of Gerar sent and took Sarah. But God came to Abimelech in a dream by night, and said to him, "Indeed you *are* a dead man because of the woman whom you have taken, for she *is* a man's wife." But Abimelech had not come near her; and he said, "Lord, will You slay a righteous nation also? "Did he not say to me, 'She *is* my sister'? And she, even she herself said, 'He *is* my brother.' In the integrity of my heart and innocence of my hands I have done this." And God said to him in a dream, "Yes, I know that you did this in the integrity of your heart. For I also withheld you from sinning against Me; therefore I did not let you touch her. "Now therefore, restore the man's wife; for he *is* a prophet, and he will pray for you and you shall live. But if you do not restore *her*, know that you shall surely die, you and all who *are* yours."

So Abimelech rose early in the morning, called all his servants, and told all these things in their hearing; and the men were very much afraid. And Abimelech called Abraham and said to him, "What have you done to us? How have I offended you, that you have brought on me and on my kingdom a great sin? You have done deeds to me that ought not to be done." Then Abimelech said to Abraham, "What did you have in view, that you have done this thing?" And Abraham said, "Because I thought, surely the fear of God *is* not in this place; and they will kill me on account of my wife. "But indeed *she is* truly my sister. She *is* the daughter of my father, but not the daughter of my mother; and she became my wife. "And it came to pass, when God caused me to wander from my father's house, that I said to her, 'This *is* your kindness that you should do for me: in every place, wherever we go, say of me, "He *is* my brother." ' " Then Abimelech took sheep, oxen, and male and female servants, and gave *them* to Abraham; and he restored Sarah his wife to him. And Abimelech said, "See, my land *is* before you; dwell where it pleases you." Then to Sarah he said, "Behold, I have given your brother a thousand *pieces* of silver; indeed this vindicates you before all who *are* with you and before everybody." Thus she was rebuked. So Abraham prayed to God; and God healed Abimelech, his wife, and his female servants. Then they bore *children*; for the LORD had closed up all the wombs of the house of Abimelech because of Sarah, Abraham's wife.

— Genesis 20:2-18 (NKJV)

The Pastor's Minute

Have you ever had something go wrong? Have you ever had a month or a year where it seemed that everything went wrong?

Did you know that there's a story in the Bible about a king who had a bad month? Everything was going wrong. In Genesis, Chapter 20, we're given five principles to apply when something's gone wrong. Here they are:

1. Stop deviating from God's moral laws. This king was about to take another man's wife which was against God's moral law.

2. Listen for God to tell you why things are going bad for you. He'll speak through a dream, a preacher's message, or a word from a caring friend.

3. Repent even if your sin was done in ignorance.

4. Make restitution. This is a faith-releasing principle that helps to purify the conscience. In other words if you stole $5, pay it back with interest. That's restitution.

5. Get someone to pray with you about the matter. King Abimelech did and God healed him, restored his family, and healed his whole nation.

"It's not my job to get other people to like me, it's my job to like other people."

"It's Not My Job!"

God's Minute

> Let each of you look out not only for his own interests, but also for the interests of others.
>
> —Philippians 2:4 (NKJV)

> But the fruit of the Spirit is love, joy, peace, longsuffering, kindness, goodness, faithfulness, gentleness, self-control. Against such there is no law.
>
> — Galatians 5:23 (NKJV)

The Pastor's Minute

Have you ever met someone who you knew didn't like you? You can feel it when someone just doesn't like you; it's like radar. It's difficult when you don't even know what you did to cause the other person to feel that way about you.

I recently heard that someone in an office where I do business didn't like me. I didn't know why. She was always respectful and seemed friendly enough, but I noticed there was always that peculiar radar. I didn't understand it. I felt like changing businesses because of this one person.

Then I went to get a haircut the other day, and my stylist, out of the blue, said she read a good quote from somewhere that day. Here it is, "It's not my job to get other people to like me; it's my job to like other people." Wow. She didn't even know about my situation, but God did, and He used her to teach me that nugget of wisdom. It's not my job to get other people to like me. It's my job to like other people.

Restructuring

God's Minute

For I know the thoughts that I think toward you,
says the LORD, thoughts of peace and not of
evil, to give you a future and a hope.

—Jeremiah 29:11 (NKJV)

The Pastor's Minute

You hear a lot about restructuring these days. Companies, businesses, churches, and even families are frequently "restructuring."

Here's a good illustration about restructuring. A Japanese company and an American company had a boat race, and the Japanese won by a mile. So the Americans hired a consultant to figure out what went wrong. The consultant reported back that the Japanese had one person managing and seven rowing while the Americans had seven managing and one rowing.

The American company immediately restructured the team. Now they had only one senior manager, six management consultants, and one rower. In the rematch, the Japanese won by two miles. So the American company fired...the rower!

Restructuring organizations, churches, and businesses won't revive them if the people's hearts and minds aren't won through positive, caring leadership and motivation.

Big Plans, Goals, And Dreams

God's Minute

For with God nothing will be impossible.

—Luke 1:37

What shall we then say to these things? If God *be* for us, who *can be* against us?

—Romans 8:31

The Pastor's Minute

Are you comfortable where you are in life, or would you like to attempt something greater than what you've already achieved? A German proverb says, "God seems pleased with those who attempt the impossible." In fact, with genuine faith, that which is impossible becomes possible.

Dr. Carl Bates reminds us to keep away from the comfortable and attempt something greater than our ability. He writes: "There came a time in my life when I earnestly prayed, 'God I want your power.'"

"Time wore on and the power did not come. One day the burden was more than I could bear. 'God, why haven't You answered that prayer?' God seemed to whisper back His simple reply, 'With plans no bigger than yours, you don't need my power.'"

Whoa! There's something to think about. What about you? Do you have plans, dreams, and goals that seem impossible? If you do, you need God's power, and when it comes, the impossible suddenly becomes possible for you.

Love Your Work

God's Minute

> The LORD God took the man and put him in
> the Garden of Eden to work it and take care of it.

—Genesis 2:15

> It is good and fitting for one to eat and drink,
> and to enjoy the good of all his labor in which he
> toils under the sun all the days of his life which
> God gives him; for it is his heritage.

—Ecclesiastes 5:18

The Pastor's Minute

Do you enjoy your work?

Ever since Adam and Eve sinned in the Garden
of Eden by disobeying God, we've been required to
work. Well...

Did you know that a link has been found between
long life and enjoying your work? It's true. A survey
conducted by NATIONS BUSINESS magazine asked

respondents to select the top ten business people America produced in the first 200 years.

Ten were selected and included Henry Ford, Alexander Graham Bell, and Thomas Edison among seven others. An interesting fact is that each of these persons were engaged in industries which are often cited in health magazines as a cause of early death. Oddly enough the average age at death for these ten nominees was nearly two decades above the national average.

The difference? These men all loved and enjoyed their work.

It's not the type of work you do but whether or not you enjoy your work that counts. This week, think of ways you can make your job more pleasant and more enjoyable. Find a way to make it more enjoyable for those you work with, and maybe you'll add a couple extra decades onto your life.

Change: Nothing To Fear

God's Minute

For God has not given us a spirit of fear, but of power and of love and of a sound mind.

—2 Timothy 1:7 (NKJV)

Though an army may encamp against me, My heart shall not fear; Though war should rise against me, In this I *will be* confident.

—Psalm 27:3 (NKJV)

The Pastor's Minute

We're living in a rapidly changing world.

Change can be frightening. In fact, I know people who are still afraid of computers. I know others who fight to keep things the same as they've always been. In fact, that's just why the religious people rejected Jesus when He came. He was different and did things in a new way.

But change can be exciting and can initiate success when it's the right kind of change.

Back in 1934, the New York Giants were losing to the Chicago Bears 10 to 3. The football field was covered with ice and the weather was bitter cold. At half time, the Giants made an unheard of change. They changed from cleats to tennis shoes. The result? They scored four touchdowns in the second half and ended up beating the Bears 30-13.

Don't be afraid of change. Don't shy away from the unconventional. Don't make the same mistake the Pharisees made when their Messiah came to them. They rejected Him because He was unconventional. Remember: changing conditions will require new methods and procedures to get the job done.

The Sin Of Gossip

God's Minute

...and a whisperer separates the best of friends.

—Proverbs 16:28

But let none of you suffer as a murderer, or *as* a thief, or *as* an evildoer, or as a busybody in other men's matters.

—1 Peter 4:15

The Pastor's Minute

Are you facing tensions at work, school, or church? The Bible tells us the cause of tension in the workplace. Gossip. That's right. Solomon said get rid of the gossiper, and tensions will cease. Very few people understand the seriousness of the sin of gossip.

Gossip separates friends.

Gossip causes tension.

If gossip is such a hideous sin, why do gossipers continue? The Bible gives us a little insight in Proverbs where it says the gossiper has a wicked heart. That's one reason. Or another reason could be that gossipers have low self-esteem and think that talking about someone else will cause themselves to be elevated. That's faulty thinking.

A gossiper is untrustworthy the Bible declares.

A gossiper is nobody's friend. But they can change if they choose, and when they do, tensions will disappear like a miracle.

How do you want to be known or remembered? As a busybody, slander-mongering gossiper? Or as one who used kind words to bless, encourage, and provide a lift to other people's day?

Creativity

God's Minute

Commit thy works unto the LORD, and thy thoughts shall be established.

—Proverbs 16:3

I wisdom dwell with prudence, and find out knowledge of witty inventions.

—Proverbs 8:12

The Pastor's Minute

Have you ever wanted to be more creative? For some, creativity seems to be a mystical gift that some have and some don't. We see designers, architects, and artists as being creative, but did you know that you too can be equally creative?

I picked up my daughter from school the other day and it was almost funny. Everybody, I mean everybody, was wearing blue jeans. It's hard to believe that blue jeans began as unsold tent canvas.

During the Goldrush in 1850, Levi Straus tried to peddle canvas to prospectors. Unsuccessful in selling canvas, he got an idea that the material could be used to make sturdy pants for the miners. Well, the rest is history. They went over big and soon were being worn by not only miners but the general public.

Creativity is God-given. It's not some dark and mysterious process. It's quite often just stepping back and looking at what already is...and asking if maybe there's a new approach you might take to reach your goals.

All He Wants Is Money

God's Minute

Bring the whole tithe into the storehouse, that there may be food in my house. Test me in this," says the LORD Almighty, "and see if I will not throw open the floodgates of heaven and pour out so much blessing that you will not have room enough for it. I will prevent pests from devouring your crops, and the vines in your fields will not cast their fruit," says the LORD Almighty.

— Malachi 3:10-11 (NIV)

The Pastor's Minute

Have you ever heard someone say, "All that preacher wants is your money!" You never hear people say, "All that tavern wants is your money." Or, "All that department store wants is your money." It's always, "All the church wants is your money."

Stop and think for a minute how that sounds. Think what it reveals about the heart of the person making such a statement. Churches help people all over the world, feeding little hungry children through mission's programs, building churches, schools, and hospitals in third world countries. And who's there when you're sick or going through a real struggle? You bet, it's the church and the wonderful pastors of our community.

When is the last time you heard about a liquor company, a theater, a manufacturer, or a night club helping the poor, feeding the hungry, or supporting an orphanage? Where do you turn when you face a crisis, like losing your home to a fire? The church... that's where.

It's sort of ironic. The institution that helps the most also gets criticized the most. Next time you hear someone make a derogatory comment about a church - any church - let them know how much the church really does for hurting humanity. Some day they may need somewhere to turn for help. And I can assure you, the churches and pastors of our community will be there for them ... even though at one time they thought all we wanted was their money.

Commitment

God's Minute

...and the two will become one flesh.' So they are no longer two, but one. Therefore what God has joined together, let man not separate.

— Mark 10:9 (NIV)

The Pastor's Minute

You don't hear much about commitment these days. I was conducting a wedding some time ago. When I told the couple that the marriage covenant is to be broken only by death, the little flower girl popped up and voiced another alternative she had heard about. "They can always get a divorce," she loudly blurted out.

Everyone laughed at the little girl's comment, but it did bring home a truth that seems to be plaguing our society today - and that's the absence of authentic commitment. A marriage covenant should be for life - "until death do us part."

Here's a story of commitment. A couple had been married for thirty years. When the husband came home, his wife was packing up. She said she'd had enough. She no longer could handle the bickering and arguing and complaining. "I'm leaving," she cried. The startled husband ran to the bedroom, pulled out a suitcase, packed his things, and ran after his wife saying, "I can't handle it anymore either. I'm going with you!"

Wow. Commitment can make a marriage fun, exciting, adventurous, and sometimes even funny.

Perfect Conditions

God's Minute

Many are the plans in a man's heart, but it is the Lord's purpose that prevails.

—Proverbs 19:21 (NIV)

The Pastor's Minute

Are you waiting for perfect conditions before you take action on your dream?

The Bible says, if you will wait for perfect conditions, you'll never get anything done.

Two old friends were sitting in a coffee shop together after being apart for a number of years. One asked the other why he had never married.

"Well, to tell you the truth, I spent all my younger years looking for the perfect woman. In San Francisco, I met a beautiful, intelligent girl with terrific eyes. But she didn't seem kind enough for me. Up in Toronto, I met a very kind lady, but we had nothing in common. Over the years, I met one woman after another who seemed just right, but I'd always discover they were missing something. Then one day I met her: intelligent, generous, kind. She had everything. She was perfect."

Puzzled, his friend, interrupted, "Why didn't you marry her?"

"Well, sad to say," he replied, "it seems she was looking for the perfect man."

Ah ha. The Bible is right. When we're looking for human perfection, we end up with nothing.

Encouragement

God's Minute

For they refreshed my spirit and yours also. Such men deserve recognition.

—1 Corinthians 16:18 (NIV)

And let us consider one another in order to stir up love and good works.

—Hebrews 10:24 (NKJV)

The Pastor's Minute

Encouragement can help people develop to their fullest potential.

When Dwight Eisenhower was a second year student at West Point Academy, he participated in the hazing activities with fellow students. One day, a Plebe accidentally ran into Eisenhower, an unpardonable offense. Dwight hollered at him, insulted him, and said, "You look like a barber."

Well, the Plebe lost his stiff composure, looked Eisenhower in the eyes, and said, "I am a barber."

Eisenhower was ashamed that he had done something stupid and unforgivable. "I've made a man ashamed of the work he did to earn a living." He vowed to never discourage or belittle anyone ever again. And he kept his vow as he led the combined Allied war machine. Even as president, he never broke his promise. He decided early on to encourage rather than discourage, and it showed in his leadership style.

The mark of a good leader, a good parent, a good boss, is the ability to encourage people to do their best.

Vince Lombardi

God's Minute

> If anyone is never at fault in what he says, he is a perfect man, able to keep his whole body in check.
>
> —James 3:2 (NIV)

> Let your conversation be always full of grace, seasoned with salt, so that you may know how to answer everyone.
>
> —Colossians 4:6 (NIV)

The Pastor's Minute

Few coaches ever demanded more from their players than did Green Bay Packers coach Vince Lombardi.

When Lombardi was seriously ill in a Washington, D.C., hospital, one of his former players, Willie Davis, flew from Los Angeles just to spend a few minutes with his coach. "I had to go," said Davis, "because that man made me feel like I was important."

People will go to the ends of the earth for someone who makes them feel important. There's something liberating about knowing that our lives really do matter and that somebody notices us and cares.

Think about it: Are there people in your life who discourage instead of encourage you? Can you talk to them about it? Or is it time for a relationship breakoff? Can you think of somebody you know who needs a little of your encouragement today? Well, what are you waiting for?

Goals

God's Minute

> Let your eyes look straight ahead, fix your gaze directly before you. Make level paths for your feet and take only ways that are firm. Do not swerve to the right or the left; keep your foot from evil.
>
> —Proverbs 4:26-27 (NIV)

> I press on toward the goal to win the prize for which God has called me heavenward in Christ Jesus.
>
> —Philippians 3:14 (NIV)

The Pastor's Minute

It seems that people with clear goals accomplish 100 to 1000 times more than people without clear goals.

When Curtis Carlson founded the Gold Bond Stamp Company in Minneapolis at the age of 24, he also set a goal of earning $100 a week - a lofty amount during the Depression. He wrote down that objective and carried it in his pocket for years until the paper was frayed. Today, Carlson companies rank among the nation's largest privately held corporations with annual revenues topping $9 billion. Goals.

While Lee Iaccoca was still in college, he set a goal of becoming vice president of Ford Motor Company before his 35th birthday. Seventeen years later, just 13 months after his self-declared deadline, it happened. Goals.

When the great architect Frank Lloyd Wright was asked at the age of 90 to single out his finest work, he answered, "My next one." Ninety years old and still laying out goals.

Have you written down your goals in life? Can you articulate your mission in life in a sentence? Are you feeling burned out in areas of your life? Maybe it would help to do as Saint Paul did: Write out your goals and dreams, and then pursue them.

Fasting

God's Minute

> When you fast, do not look somber as the hypo-
> crites do, for they disfigure their faces to show
> men they are fasting. I tell you the truth, they
> have received their reward in full. But when
> you fast, put oil on your head and wash your
> face, so that it will not be obvious to men that
> you are fasting, but only to your Father, who is
> unseen; and your Father, who sees what is done
> in secret, will reward you.
>
> — Matthew 6:17-18 (NIV)

The Pastor's Minute

Have you ever thought about fasting? I'd read
about fasting in the Bible but always thought it was
kind of an "iffy" thing. You know, you can do it "if"
you want, but you don't have to. So, I never fasted
much.

Then I started reading about people who practiced fasting regularly. In other words, they would go a day, or three days, or seven days without food, drinking only distilled water. Wow. The results were more than just spiritual.

Some had a complete rejuvenation of health and vitality. Others slowed down the aging process. All eliminated body toxins, some conquered allergies, others had their acne problems clear up, some defeated sinus problems, normalized their blood pressure, brought their cholesterol and homocysteine levels down. Some claimed boosted energy levels and even the breaking of demonic forces.

Medical doctor Ronald G. Cridland said, "Fasting can save your life."

I've decided that I'm going to fast more this year. And of course, check with your doctor first to see how much fasting you can do before you begin. You can get a copy of my book, "The Miracle Results Of Fasting," with 92 power-packed pages by calling (517) 321-CARE. See how this practice can rejuvenate your life and bring you continual health.

Fasting Benefits

God's Minute

> Then your light will break forth like the dawn, and your healing will quickly appear; then your righteousness will go before you, and the glory of the LORD will be your rear guard. Then you will call, and the LORD will answer; you will cry for help, and he will say: Here am I. If you do away with the yoke of oppression, with the pointing finger and malicious talk, and if you spend yourselves in behalf of the hungry and satisfy the needs of the oppressed, then your light will rise in the darkness, and your night will become like the noonday.

— Isaiah 58:9-10 (NIV)

The Pastor's Minute

Last time we were together, I talked to you about this strange practice of fasting. Many have had questions and even raised eyebrows about this subject of fasting, so I would like to elaborate.

What if you could do something that would bring amazing blessings to your life, would cost you nothing, and would hurt no one? Blessings like:

- Deliverance from bad habits

- Revelations from God

- Divine protection

- Quickly answered prayers

- Speedy return of your health

- A constant supply of your needs

Would you want to receive blessings like these? The Bible promises them, in Isaiah 58, to the person who will practice fasting. In other words, go without food for a day, maybe two or three or more days drinking just water (preferably distilled).

Dr. Dean Ornish said that after only twelve hours of fasting, your body begins to cleanse itself of harmful toxins, the kind that cause diseases down the road. He said that in twelve hours, your body begins to repair itself.

Why not try it this year? Maybe once a week or twice a week. See what happens. Remember to check with your doctor first.

"Pa"

God's Minute

The LORD will guide you always; he will satisfy your needs in a sun-scorched land and will strengthen your frame. You will be like a well-watered garden, like a spring whose waters never fail.

—Isaiah 58:11 (NIV)

The Pastor's Minute

Fasting. What an interesting topic. I hate it, but I know it's good for me.

Years ago, there was a man named "Pa." He was my great grandfather. At the age of 81, he was diagnosed with cancer. He was given an ultimatum: Have surgery, and maybe you'll live; don't have the surgery and die within months.

Well, Pa was a stubborn man. He decided not to have the surgery. Instead, he went on a modified fast. He quit eating meats and ate only boiled vegetables and fruits and strange things like boiled rhubarb. He felt great and worked on his little farm in what appeared to be great health for 16 more years.

He died at the age of 97 and not from cancer. Could it be that Pa discovered the miracle secret of what the Bible has taught all along? That fasting will cause your health to spring forth speedily? I don't know, but I do know that I became a believer in the practice of regular fasting. In fact, it was my doctor who first suggested it to me.

Do you need your health to spring forth speedily? You should check with your doctor and see if you can fast to the extent that you are able. You may see some miracles.

Bible Prophecy

God's Minute

> Nation will rise against nation, and kingdom against kingdom. There will be famines and earthquakes in various places. All these are the beginning of birth pains. "Then you will be handed over to be persecuted and put to death, and you will be hated by all nations because of me. At that time many will turn away from the faith and will betray and hate each other, and many false prophets will appear and deceive many people. Because of the increase of wickedness, the love of most will grow cold, but he who stands firm to the end will be saved.
>
> —Matthew 24:7-13 (NIV)

The Pastor's Minute

Have you ever wondered where we are on the prophetic calendar? The signs of the return of Christ in a nutshell are:

1. Focus on the Middle East

2. Religious deception and an occultic revolution (psychics, astrologers, etc.)

3. Wars and rumors of wars as it relates to Israel

4. Social and political chaos, scandals, and such

5. Famines in various parts of the world

6. Violence and terrorism

7. Great technological advances

8. Multiplied family problems

9. Increased demonic activity

10. Genuine God-sent revival

These are just ten of the signs. You can call (517) 321-CARE to get a copy of my book, "End Times Bible Prophecy," if you're interested in more. The question is: Are we now living in the end times? If so, are we ready to meet the Lord? After He comes, it'll be too late.

Travel

God's Minute

> But Daniel, keep this prophecy a secret; seal it up so that it will not be understood until the end times, when travel and education shall be vastly increased!

—Daniel 12:4 (TLB)

The Pastor's Minute

Another sign of the times. We've been looking at a fascinating subject: Bible Prophecy. When will Christ come back?

The prophet Daniel gave us another clue. He said as we near the end, "Travel will vastly increase."

Today, U.S. citizens alone spend $32.9 billion on international travel.

In 1947, only 7 million people traveled by air. Today, 550 million people are traveling by air.

In fact, the Dallas airport alone is now planning for 60 million air travelers a year.

I guess you could say that we are living in a day when travel has vastly increased. Who knows? Maybe this will be the year Jesus comes back. He promised He will. And He's never lied.

Are you ready for His return?

High Risk

God's Minute

For nation shall rise against nation, and kingdom against kingdom: and there shall be famines, and pestilences, and earthquakes, in divers
places. All these *are* the beginning of sorrows.
Then shall they deliver you up to be afflicted,
and shall kill you: and ye shall be hated of all
nations for my name's sake.

—Matthew 24:7-9 (KJV)

The Pastor's Minute

We've been looking at Bible prophecy.

When will Jesus come back? Well, Saint Paul said
it would be during perilous times. In other words, it
would be during a day of high risks.

Is this the high risk time Saint Paul talked about
in his letter to Timothy?

Did you read where 100 people were infected with HIV by one man in a matter of just a few months? High risk days, I'd say.

The World Health Organization revised its figures recently and now says that within two years, over 110 million will be infected with the high risk AIDS virus.

According to one report, there are now over 2000 off-beat cults operating in America that claim 10 million members. Pretty high risk religious times too, it seems.

Some cults offer to tutor your children for free. Then they spend their time indoctrinating them in some religious goobly-gook that can do nothing but hurt your kids later on. Pretty high risk times, it seems to me.

Could this be the last generation? Maybe. Things are getting more high risk all the time. I hope you're not risking your eternity with some strange idea about God. Find the real God in the Bible.

Rapture

God's Minute

Watch ye therefore, and pray always, that ye may be accounted worthy to escape all these things that shall come to pass, and to stand before the Son of man.

—Luke 21:36

Then we which are alive *and* remain shall be caught up together with them in the clouds, to meet the Lord in the air: and so shall we ever be with the Lord.

—1 Thessalonians 4:17

The Pastor's Minute

People are very interested in Bible prophecy these days. Because of the high interest, I thought I'd talk further about Prophecy.

Have you ever heard about the Rapture? It's a mysterious event that could take place at any moment. The Rapture is "Harpazo" in the Greek language and it means "to be suddenly, supernaturally snatched away."

It's the event when millions of Christians will be supernaturally transported off the earth. They'll just disappear. The earth will then go into seven years of serious judgments. Animals will lose their natural fear of man, demons will be loosed, insects will carry painful stings, tumors and sores will appear on people, meteorites with vapor trails will scream across the earth, and water will turn to blood and poison (probably from biological warfare). In fact, in a short seven years after the rapture, only one fourth of the earth's population will be able to survive.

The way out? The Rapture. There are two categories: Those who are ready and those who are not. Those who are ready will go for the ride of their lives. Those who are not? ...Well, we don't even want to think about that.

More On Bible Prophecy

God's Minute

> Watch therefore: for ye know not what hour your
> Lord doth come. But know this, that if the
> goodman of the house had known in what watch
> the thief would come, he would have watched,
> and would not have suffered his house to be
> broken up. Therefore be ye also ready: for in
> such an hour as ye think not the Son of man
> cometh.
>
> —Matthew 24:42-44

The Pastor's Minute

It seems there's a lot of interest in Bible prophecy
these days. I received my copy of the U.S. News and
World Report, and behold, on the cover were the
words, "Prophecy: Religious scholars' new insight
into predictions about the second coming and the end
of the world." Interesting, and a pretty good write-
up.

It seems that 66 percent of Americans believe that Jesus Christ will one day return. Well, after all, He promised He would. And He even, through the prophets, told us what the world conditions would be just before He would come.

He said the focus would be on the Middle Eastern nations, especially Israel. Well, watch the news every night, and there will be something about Israel there.

He said there'd be famines. There always have been, but now one third of the world's population goes to bed hungry, and tens of thousands are dying daily of starvation. Those ads you see on TV of starving children are true.

And He said a lot more. It sort of looks like this could be it. We may be at the end of the wire now. Jesus said in Matthew 25, "Those who are ready will go in, the others will be left behind." I hope you're ready.

Humbling The Proud

God's Minute

But he giveth more grace. Wherefore he saith,
God resisteth the proud, but giveth grace unto
the humble.

—James 4:6

Pride *goeth* before destruction, and an haughty
spirit before a fall.

—Proverbs 16:18

The Pastor's Minute

Do you know people who feel it's their call in life
to set everyone else straight? The Bible says that God
will humble the proud but exalt the humble. The
proud person is always trying to set others straight
but never seems to see his or her own particular faults.

I've always felt, that as a pastor, it's better to feed
the sheep than to try to pick off their lice.

197

A lady came to South Africa to set a church straight. She didn't know that particular church was already feeding 2,000 homeless people a day. She picked up a little boy off the street and carried him to the front of the church and told the people that they should be caring for people like little "Stempie." That really was his name. What she didn't know was that the pastor sang lullabies to little Stempie in front of the church each evening. As she rebuked the people for not caring more, little Stempie's pants fell down as she was holding him. He was mooning the whole congregation, only she didn't know it!

It's true. God humbles the proud, but exalts the humble. Please don't feel that it's your call to set everyone straight. It's better to be a feeder than a lice picker.

Attitudes

God's Minute

> The thoughts of the diligent *tend* only to plente-
> ousness; but of every one *that is* hasty only to
> want.

—Proverbs 21:5

The Pastor's Minute

Do you know how important your attitude is to your success? I recently spent a couple of weeks ministering in South Africa. I met a failing pastor who said that he just can't be successful in South Africa because he doesn't have any American support. He really believes he can't do anything without American support, so he continues in his failure.

Then I met Neville McDonald, a pastor of several thousand people in Constantia, South Africa. Neville has his main church, and three satellite churches; he feeds two thousand people a day and ministers in crusades around the world. I asked him how much American support he's had. He responded with a smile, "None."

So here's one guy, a failure, because his attitude says he needs a handout.

And here's another guy, who never took a handout, just put his hand to the plow. He believes that with God all things are possible, and he's succeeding.

Attitude. It makes all the difference in the world.

How is your attitude today?

Affirmative Achievement

God's Minute

> When a servant comes in from plowing or taking care of sheep, he doesn't just sit down and eat, but first prepares his master's meal and serves him his supper before he eats his own. And he is not even thanked, for he is merely doing what he is supposed to do. Just so, if you merely obey me, you should not consider yourselves worthy of praise. For you have simply done your duty!
>
> — Luke 17:10 (TLB)

The Pastor's Minute

Some people need constant acknowledgment and affirmation. Some folks, usually the low achievers in life, are always looking for recognition, acknowledgment, affirmation, and appreciation. If they don't get it the way they should, they're mad and miserable.

Why can't we just do things because they're right without thinking that we need to be appreciated? Why can't we simply put our hand to the plow and move ahead, achieving in life without worrying about somebody recognizing us or giving us the desired affirmation? High achievers don't worry about being acknowledged, recognized, appreciated, or affirmed. They just do what they feel called to do to fulfill their purpose in life, and generally speaking, they're happy people.

The ones who are always ticked off because they weren't recognized or appreciated are usually the sad sacks that moan and groan through life without ever accomplishing much worthwhile. They were too busy thinking about all the honors they deserved instead of achieving something of significance.

How about you? Do you desire affirmation? Or do you want to be an achiever? It's your choice.

Correction

God's Minute

Whoso loveth instruction loveth knowledge: but he that hateth reproof *is* brutish.

—Proverbs 12:1

The man who is often reproved but refuses to accept criticism will suddenly be broken and never have another chance.

—Proverbs 29:1 (TLB)

The Pastor's Minute

Do you know someone who refuses to be corrected? I think we've all known people who refuse to admit their mistakes. When you lovingly try to correct them, they make a thousand excuses of why they are the way they are. When you offer them a helpful suggestion, the defenses go up, the excuses pour out, and the "yeah, buts" begin. Sometimes they'll even tell you they don't want to be corrected.

To help them spell out a word correctly or point out a better way seems to wound their sensitive self-esteem.

The Bible says the one who refuses to accept correction will suddenly be broken and never have another chance.

When someone wants to help you through correction or constructive criticism, simply say, "Thanks, I appreciate your thoughtfulness in helping me." Don't put up the defensive barrier and begin to make excuses and get mad. After all, this could be your last chance.

Evolution

God's Minute

> In the beginning God created the heaven and
> the earth.
>
> —Genesis 1:1

The Pastor's Minute

An interesting thing happened to my little airplane the other day. My little Cessna Skyhawk airplane, after many years, suddenly, through a freak act of nature, became a Boeing 727. Then my little shed out back, one day through some sort of transmutation, was transformed into a glimmering mansion. I was amazed.

Right! If you believe those stories, you're probably making some interesting investments in swamp land right now.

Of course nobody believes that a four seat Cessna can evolve into a Boeing 727. Nobody believes that an old tool shed can evolve into a priceless mansion. I don't think anybody really believes they evolved from monkeys which evolved from fish which evolved from a single-celled blob of goo that came from who knows where.

Deep down, you and I both know we were created by a loving Creator and, therefore, are accountable to Him. When we violate His laws, and we all have, that's called sin. When we sin, it brings death to our lives. That's why we need a savior. I'm grateful that our creator sent Jesus with the only plan to save us from our sins and get us into Heaven.

Criticism

God's Minute

The student shares his teacher's fate. The servant shares his master's! And since I, the master of the household have been called 'Satan,' how much more will you! But don't be afraid of those who threaten you. For the time is coming when the truth will be revealed: their secret plots will become public information.

—Matthew 10: 25, 26 (TLB)

For we are not fighting against people made of flesh and blood, but against persons without bodies - the evil rulers of the unseen world, those mighty satanic beings and great evil princes of darkness who rule this world; and against huge numbers of wicked spirits in the spirit world.

—Ephesians 6:12 (TLB)

The Pastor's Minute

All of us have faced criticism and it's not pleasant. While we're growing up, a lot of us spend a great deal of time worrying about what the world thinks of us. By the time we reach 50, we realize that the world wasn't paying much attention. But what do you do in the meantime when you find yourself under a critical attack?

1. Understand the difference between destructive and constructive criticism.

2. Don't take yourself too seriously.

3. Look beyond the criticism, and see the critic. Who said it? Do you respect them? Do they continually criticize others? Are they helping you?

4. Watch your attitude toward the critic. Don't become like him or her.

5. Realize that good people are always criticized. They called Jesus a glutton, a drunkard, a demon-possessed friend of sinners.

6. Don't allow the critic to get you off course. If you're being criticized, more than likely you're doing something right.

Overload

God's Minute

Be careful for nothing; but in every thing by prayer and supplication with thanksgiving let your requests be made known unto God. And the peace of God, which passeth all understanding, shall keep your hearts and minds through Christ Jesus.

—Philippians 4:6-7

The Pastor's Minute

Have you ever felt like you're in a hurry all over? Last week I arrived home from a nine-day business trip. My desk at home was piled with work and bills to pay. My desk at the office had stacks of work to accomplish. My phone was ringing constantly with people in serious need. I had meetings, appointments, emergencies. I was about ready to scream. I had a hurried and frustrated feeling all over. It was like I had to be in five places at once, so I decided to pray.

"Lord, what's wrong here? I have no peace. And this Sunday, I'm preaching on peace." It seemed that the Lord answered me and said, "Dave, you can't carry 10,000 tons over a bridge rated for 10 tons."

It was then I realized that each day is like a ten-ton bridge. We can only carry so much. If we try to drag yesterday's and tomorrow's load over today's bridge we have a collapse. Cut yesterday's load. It's gone. Disconnect tomorrow's load, and take it one step at a time. What you can't handle throw on the Lord. He said to cast your cares upon Him because He cares for you. I did it, and wow, I sure felt a lot better.

Your Purpose

God's Minute

> Just as each of us has one body with many members, and these members do not all have the same function, so in Christ we who are many form one body, and each member belongs to all the others. We have different gifts, according to the grace given us. If a man's gift is prophesying, let him use it in proportion to his faith. If it is serving, let him serve; if it is teaching, let him teach; if it is encouraging, let him encourage; if it is contributing to the needs of others, let him give generously; if it is leadership, let him govern diligently; if it is showing mercy, let him do it cheerfully.
>
> —Romans 12:4-8 (NIV)

The Pastor's Minute

What's the one thing you really do well and enjoy doing? Maybe that's your calling in life. I know people who aren't really doing what they'd like to be doing because they have fifteen years in at the workplace and feel they should stay until they retire.

But, you know, you'll only really be happy when you've found that special niche in life. That special something you really enjoy. My daughter's a real ham. She loves radio and television, so she's going to school to learn broadcasting and broadcast journalism. That's what she loves. She does well in it, but give her a math problem and she bombs.

I know a fellow who is retired, but he loves driving around on the highways so he can find people who need help - a flat tire, a broken engine, an overheated radiator. He loves fixing things for people. The five percent of people who *do* find their special niche are balanced, healthy, emotionally fulfilled individuals.

Jesus knew His purpose. That's why He didn't build a mall or even a synagogue. He never wrote a book, didn't even empty out all the hospitals. He stuck to His purpose. You can, too.

Afraid Of Preachers

God's Minute

Love is patient, love is kind. It does not envy, it does not boast, it is not proud. It is not rude, it is not self-seeking, it is not easily angered, it keeps no record of wrongs. Love does not delight in evil but rejoices with the truth. It always protects, always trusts, always hopes, always perseveres. Love never fails.

—1 Corinthians 13:4-8 (NIV)

The Pastor's Minute

Some folks are afraid of preachers, and frankly, I can't blame them.

One day a guest preacher was preaching his heart out at a revival meeting. The only problem was the wireless microphone wasn't working, so he had to use one of those old microphones that hangs around your neck and has a cord attached. Well, he'd walk around on the platform until he ran out of cord and was almost choked. This tug of war happened several times throughout the service.

Finally, he raised his voice, lunged forward to make a point, and lifted his fist in the air. A frightened little girl leaned close to her mother, looked up and asked, "Mommy, will he hurt us if he gets loose?"

Don't worry, I won't get loose. And I probably won't yell at you either. So be sure to join us this Sunday, and start the week right. If you aren't in the Lansing, Michigan area, be sure to spend time in God's house this week wherever you live. You'll be glad you did.

Small Beginnings

God's Minute

Though thy beginning was small, yet thy latter end should greatly increase.

—Job 8:7

Do not despise this small beginning, for the eyes of the Lord rejoice to see the work begin...

—Zechariah 4:10 (TLB)

The Pastor's Minute

Despise not the day of small beginnings. That's a Bible verse.

The word "despise" means to disrespect or be ashamed of. Many people think they can't accomplish much in life because they have so little to work with. They're ashamed to start small. Yet God seems pleased with those who take what little they have, dedicate it to Him, and start doing something.

A little is a lot when God is with you.

Think of it. Jesus was born in a little town - not a big city. He rode into Jerusalem on a little donkey - not a giant steed. God loves to do great things when we take our little and let Him turn it into a lot.

My ministry began as a little home Bible study with just a few people. Today, over 6,000 call me their pastor. Jim Russell, founder of the multimillion dollar Russell Business Forms (RBF), started his business from a little corner in his house. A little can become a lot when God is with you.

Why not take your little, dedicate it to God, start doing something, and watch your little become a lot?

Greed

God's Minute

> But godliness with contentment is great gain. For we brought nothing into *this* world, *and it is* certain we can carry nothing out. And having food and raiment let us be therewith content. But they that will be rich fall into temptation and a snare, and *into* many foolish and hurtful lusts, which drown men in destruction and perdition. For the love of money is the root of all evil: which while some coveted after, they have erred from the faith, and pierced themselves through with many sorrows. But thou, O man of God, flee these things; and follow after righteousness, godliness, faith, love, patience, meekness.

—1 Timothy 6:6-11

The Pastor's Minute

People can be greedy. In fact, you've probably even heard someone talk about those greedy preachers. Well, here's a story from the Houston Post that gives an important lesson about greed.

A young man from a wealthy family was graduating from high school and expected his father to buy him a car as a graduation gift. At the graduation party, his father handed him a package. He opened it and it was a Bible. The young man was so mad, he threw down the Bible, stormed out of the house, and never spoke to his dad again.

The father died a few years later. When the son was going through his father's belongings, he found the Bible he had thrown down in his anger. He brushed the dust off, opened its pages, and there was a cashier's check for the price of a new car dated on his graduation day.

God's greatest gifts are still found in the pages of God's Word, the Bible. But we sometimes allow greed to destroy relationships and divert our attention from the real treasures in life.

Don't let this happen to you. Focus on the treasures in your life today.

Synergy

God's Minute

> And if a kingdom be divided against itself, that kingdom cannot stand. And if a house be divided against itself, that house cannot stand.

> —Mark 3:25

The Pastor's Minute

Let me ask you a question. Where you work, is there a real commitment to teamwork and unity, or is it a gossiping, backbiting, "You do your job and I'll do mine," or "You do your job and you do mine too" sort of place?

An experiment was done at a county fair a few years ago during the horse-pulling contest that illustrates the value of teamwork. The winning horse, by himself pulled 4,500 pounds. But when they hooked both horses up together, they pulled 12,000 pounds.

Together, they pulled 3,500 pounds more than the total amount they could pull separately. It's called synergy. One or more working harmoniously together can accomplish 25 to 100 percent more than the total of everyone working separately. That means more productivity, more fun at work, and more money over the course of time.

Those who refuse to work on the team are costing you dearly. Here's the principle: Teamwork divides the effort but multiplies the results.

Life After Death

God's Minute

Jesus saith unto him, I am the way, the truth, and the life: no man cometh unto the Father, but by me.

—John 14:6

And as it is appointed unto men once to die, but after this the judgment: So Christ was once offered to bear the sins of many; and unto them that look for him shall he appear the second time without sin unto salvation.

—Hebrews 9:27-28

The Pastor's Minute

There was an interesting article in Omni magazine about Dr. Maurice Rawlings, a cardiologist, who is constantly treating emergency patients, many of whom have near-death experiences.

It is not unusual for Dr. Rawlings to hear those people speak of seeing a bright light, lush green meadows, and rows of smiling relatives, along with a deep sense of peace. But he also said that nearly 50 percent of the near-death patients he interviewed spoke of fire and devil-like creatures and other horrible sights reflecting the darkness and terror of hell.

"Just listening to these patients has changed my whole life," claims Dr. Rawlings. "There is a life after death, and if I don't know where I'm going, then it's not safe to die."

Those are the words of the cardiologist who interviewed over 300 near-death patients who saw the world beyond.

Can you be sure of where you're going after this life is over? Is it safe for you to die? Jesus promised eternal life and Heaven for all those who trust in Him alone.

As Good As It Gets

God's Minute

> Therefore, since we have been justified through faith, we have peace with God through our Lord Jesus Christ, through whom we have gained access by faith into this grace in which we now stand. And we rejoice in the hope of the glory of God.

—Romans 5:2 (NIV)

> I have come that they may have life, and have it to the full.

—John 10:10b (NIV)

The Pastor's Minute

Have you see the movie "As Good As It Gets" with Jack Nicholson and Helen Hunt? I love the part where Helen Hunt is whining to Jack Nicholson, "I just want a normal boyfriend." At that point, her mother, who was secretly listening, popped her head out and said, "That's what everyone wants, dear. They don't exist."

It's true; everyone, it seems, wants something that doesn't exist.

Everyone wants the ideal job; but it doesn't exist.

Everyone wants the perfect marriage; but it doesn't exist.

Churchgoers look for a perfect pastor; but he doesn't exist.

Is this as good as it gets? Well, it is until you first come to make peace with imperfection, and second, make peace with the only perfect One who ever existed - God. When you do these two things, you'll no longer ask, "Is this as good as it gets?" Instead you'll be asking, "How can it get any better?"

Hurts

God's Minute

Praise be to the Lord, to God our Savior, who daily bears our burdens.

—Psalms 68:19 (NIV)

Come to me, all you who are weary and burdened, and I will give you rest.

—Matthew 11:28 (NIV)

The Pastor's Minute

Have you ever hurt so bad that you couldn't think straight, your stomach was all knotted up, and you wondered if any hope was left in the world for you? Well, I've felt that way, and I understand what you're going through.

Maybe it's a bitter divorce, a painful financial reversal, or a wayward child who has gotten in with the wrong crowd. Perhaps you've lost a loved one or even a job, and you don't know where to turn. Believe me, I meet people who face these torturous struggles every week.

Jesus made a promise to anyone facing these vicissitudes of life. He said, "Come unto me, and I'll give you rest." (That is relief.) He's promised to make us each "more than a winner." But we have to come to Him.

Be sure to spend time in God's house this week and be introduced to the One who untangles the messes and hurts of life.

Blaming Others

God's Minute

If we confess our sins, he is faithful and just to forgive us *our* sins, and to cleanse us from all unrighteousness.

—1 John 1:9

The Pastor's Minute

Why is it that we like to blame others for all our mistakes and troubles? I heard the other day that there is a computer out now that's so human that when it makes a mistake, it blames another machine.

I guess it goes back to Adam and Eve when they first sinned. Adam said, "It was the woman's fault!" Then Eve turned around and blamed the devil. But the fact is, we all make our own choices in the end, and our choices have consequences.

Successful people don't waste time blaming things on other people. They don't say, "It's my wife's fault" or "My husband made me do it, or my boss, or my teacher or anybody else." Successful people understand that responsibility is one of the first keys to true success.

It's a liberating day when we quit blaming and simply say, "I messed up. I'm responsible. I'm sorry."

Fuelers And Drainers

God's Minute

Reckless words pierce like a sword, but the tongue of the wise brings healing.

—Proverbs 12:18 (NIV)

Like the coolness of snow at harvest time is a trustworthy messenger to those who send him; he refreshes the spirit of his masters.

—Proverbs 25:13 (NIV)

The Pastor's Minute

Have you ever seen somebody coming your way when suddenly everything in you started screaming, "RUN!"?

If you've had that experience, it's probably because that other person is a drainer. They drain you with their never-ending complaints, their boring monologue, their money problems; they don't bring their lunch so they want part of yours; they're typically upset and usually bring a barrage of bad news. They leave you drained.

On the other hand, there are those I call "fuelers." They're upbeat, positive, full of faith and motivation, and you feel good when they're around. Fuelers add something to your life; they give you fuel. Drainers, well, they just drain you.

Life is made up of fuelers and drainers. Fuelers are loved and appreciated. Drainers are, at best, just tolerated. Be a fueler; not a drainer.

Psychic Lines

God's Minute

> Call to me and I will answer you and tell you great and unsearchable things you do not know.
>
> —Jeremiah 33:3 (NIV)

> "For I know the plans I have for you," declares the LORD, "plans to prosper you and not to harm you, plans to give you hope and a future."
>
> —Jeremiah 29:11 (NIV)

The Pastor's Minute

What about all these psychic lines? Did you hear about the psychic line that went bankrupt? They just didn't see it coming. And the psychic fair that had to be canceled due to unforeseen weather conditions?

A fellow called a psychic who told him that he'd be poor and unhappy until he was 30. "Well, then what?" he asked. The psychic responded, "Then you'll get used to it." Wow, what a prediction.

One recent year the psychic predictions in the tabloids were almost 100 percent wrong. Nothing happened that they predicted. But people still spend money on 900 numbers and papers with horoscopes. Why is it? Well, I think it's because we all want to know the right decisions to make, and we want to know a little about the future. But most folks don't realize that God Himself has promised these very things to anyone who would call on Him. And He doesn't have a 900 number.

Just talk to Him. It's free, and He's waiting to hear from you and show you wonderful things.

Never Been To Church

God's Minute

> For God so loved the world, that he gave his only begotten Son, that whosoever believeth in him should not perish, but have everlasting life. For God sent not his Son into the world to condemn the world; but that the world through him might be saved.
>
> —John 3:17

> Behold, I stand at the door, and knock: if any man hear my voice, and open the door, I will come in to him, and will sup with him, and he with me.
>
> —Revelation 3:20

The Pastor's Minute

Here's an interesting true story.

A couple of weeks ago, a young lady walked up to me at the mall. Recognizing me, she asked an interesting question, "Can someone come to your church if they're not a member?" "Well, of course," I replied, "we always give visitors a grand welcome." Most churches in our community do.

She went on to tell me that she had never been to church and never owned a Bible. So, we invited her to church and went out and got her a Bible along with a copy of my book, "The Secret of Power with God, How to Tap Into the Unlimited Resources of God."

Well, a few days later, my daughter saw this young lady again.

She said she had started reading the book, and when she came to chapter three, she prayed for the first time in her life. She said she asked Jesus to come into her life and then went on to say what a powerful and positive difference it has made in her life.

God wants to make a difference in your life too. Don't wait until someone invites you to church. Stop in this Sunday. You'll get a big welcome, I'm sure, whatever church you decide to visit. Maybe, just maybe, God will give you the miracle you've been looking for.

Success 101

God's Minute

Keep therefore the words of this covenant, and do them, that ye may prosper in all that ye do.

—Deuteronomy 29:9

...in all these things we are more than conquerors through him that loved us.

—Romans 8:37

The Pastor's Minute

You want to be successful, I know. Everybody wants to be successful. I never heard a businessman say, "I hope my business goes bankrupt." I never heard an athlete say, "I sure hope I lose." And I never heard a young couple entering into marriage say, "We hope our marriage ends in hurt and divorce."

No, everyone starts out with the dream to be successful in whatever endeavor they embark upon. What is the real key to success?

Well, Jesus summed it up in Matthew Chapter 5 in the Bible. He gathered his disciples to give them their first lesson in success. Some call it the beatitudes. I call it Success 101. He promised that if we would follow the principles He outlined, we would be blessed, happy, and have special advantages and benefits that would give our life an edge.

You can get the best out of life. You can win over every circumstance and situation. You can discover that your life is worthwhile when you follow the blueprint Jesus gave. Read Matthew Chapter 5 as we continue to look at the Success 101 teachings.

Beatitude #1

God's Minute

> Trust in the LORD with all thine heart; and lean
> not unto thine own understanding. In all thy
> ways acknowledge him, and he shall direct thy
> paths.
>
> —Proverbs 3:6

> Blessed *are* the poor in spirit: for theirs is the
> kingdom of heaven.
>
> —Matthew 5:3

The Pastor's Minute

Hello, my dear friend. We are taking a look at Principles of Success 101.

Jesus said, "Blessed are the poor in spirit." To be blessed means to be overflowing with happiness and special divine advantages in life. It means you'll live life to the fullest.

Now, there's nothing particularly blessed about being poor. Being broke doesn't make you happy nor does it give you any special advantages in life.

Jesus wasn't referring to the financially disabled. He said, "Blessed are the poor in spirit." What does that mean? Simply this:

1. It means to be humble enough to be taught - teachability. Know-it-alls are not blessed.

2. It means to admit one's personal inadequacies. Face up to the fact that none of us are an island. We need others.

3. It means to trust God in every area of our lives where we are inadequate.

A farmer knows that low land is easier to irrigate than high land. And a humble, teachable person is easier to bless than a proud, arrogant person.

Which are you?

Beatitude #2

God's Minute

> Blessed *are* they that mourn: for they shall be comforted.
>
> —Matthew 5:4

> Be careful for nothing; but in every thing by prayer and supplication with thanksgiving let your requests be made known unto God. And the peace of God, which passeth all understanding, shall keep your hearts and minds through Christ Jesus.
>
> —Philippians 4:6-7

The Pastor's Minute

Do you want to have special advantages in life?

Last time I shared with you the first principle of success: Humility and Teachability. Let's look at the next one. "Blessed are they that mourn."

Sounds contradictory. If you mourn, you'll be happy. Strange, but Jesus wasn't talking about those who live a life of sorrow and grief. If you look more closely, you'll find that he was referring to a condition connected with prayer.

When we are sad about our sins and mourn over the hurts many people are facing in the world and we go to pray about them, Boom - happiness will come to our souls, and supernatural benefits will come to our lives opening the door to greater success.

I'm sure you could use some happiness in your soul and supernatural benefits in your life. Make sure today that your sins have been forgiven. If you haven't taken that step yet, the happiness and benefits will always seem just out of your reach. Turn everything over to Jesus today and watch your life change for the better, and experience those supernatural benefits God's promised to those who mourn in prayer.

Beatitude #3

God's Minute

> Blessed *are* the meek: for they shall inherit the earth.
>
> —Matthew 5:5

> But the fruit of the Spirit is love, joy, peace, longsuffering, gentleness, goodness, faith, Meekness, temperance: against such there is no law.
>
> —Galatians 5:23

The Pastor's Minute

How would you like to have more real estate?

Believe it or not, Jesus promised real estate to those who would develop the success principle called meekness. He said, "Blessed are the meek for they shall inherit the earth." That is soil, real estate.

Can this be true? It's hard to swallow, but Jesus said it.

What does meekness mean? It doesn't mean to be weak and a doormat for others. Essentially, the word "meek" means this:

1. To realize you're not perfect and neither is anyone else

2. To be unselfish and unassuming

3. To be gentle and unobtrusive

4. To be sensitive and gracious toward others

5. To have a sensitive posture toward God and His will

That's meekness. It will bless you here and now, and also into eternity. When we develop the five qualities of meekness, get ready; we're going to get some real estate.

Beatitude #4

God's Minute

And Jesus said unto them, I am the bread of life: he that cometh to me shall never hunger; and he that believeth on me shall never thirst.

—John 6:35

But seek ye first the kingdom of God, and his righteousness; and all these things shall be added unto you.

—Matthew 6:33

The Pastor's Minute

Success 101. Some call it The Beatitudes.

We've looked at three principles of success. Let's look at number four.

Jesus said, "Blessed are they which do hunger and thirst after righteousness."

When mother Theresa visited America, she made an interesting comment. She observed, "In India, people are dying of physical hunger. In America, people are dying of spiritual hunger."

It's true. That's why Jesus said you're going to have special advantages and benefits in life if you hunger and thirst after righteousness. What did He mean? Simply this: If you have an appetite for spiritual things and put those things first, He'll see to it that all the things others are thirsting for (like popularity, success, and financial freedom) will come to you instead. When you develop an appetite for reading your Bible and attending church, God will give you supernatural ideas on how to gain the other things.

Success 101 principle: Cultivate an appetite for spiritual things.

Cut Me A Break

God's Minute

It is of the LORD'S mercies that we are not consumed, because his compassions fail not. They are new every morning: great is thy faithfulness.

—Lamentations 3:23

Blessed *are* the merciful: for they shall obtain mercy.

—Matthew 5:7

The Pastor's Minute

Have you ever wished someone would cut you a break? We've been talking about Success 101 or what is commonly called The Beatitudes. Today we look at Number Five: Blessed are the merciful for they shall be given mercy.

What does it mean to be merciful? It's a sense of pity toward others and a desire to somehow relieve someone else's misery. It's a kind, non-retaliating spirit that refuses to return evil for evil.

The opposite of mercy is anger, vengeance, revenge, the get-even attitude.

The Bible tells us that if we develop this success principle called mercy:

1. We'll receive leniency ourselves when we mess up

2. We'll be honored

3. We'll nourish our own soul

4. Happiness will be ours

Think of someone who needs your mercy this week. Act on it, and you'll be blessed yourself.

Blaming

God's Minute

> Have mercy on me, O God, according to your unfailing love; according to your great compassion blot out my transgressions. Wash away all my iniquity and cleanse me from my sin.
>
> —Psalm 51:1-2 (NIV)

The Pastor's Minute

I once knew a man whom I'll call George. George had a real problem with alcohol and drugs. It wrecked his marriage, destroyed his family, cost him job after job, but of course, it was never George's fault. It was his wife's or his boss's or something that happened to George when he was young.

It's normal for individuals whose world is falling apart to look for another person on whom they can transfer the blame. It's a natural human instinct to transfer blame, but it's self-destructive. Maybe life did deal George a lousy hand; but it was George's own decision to drink and to take those drugs. The fact is, George's world didn't fall apart because he was a victim but because he made wrong choices.

And his situation would never have turned around if George hadn't stopped blaming others and hadn't accepted the responsibility for his own actions and then given his life to God who still is in the business of doing miracles and changing people's lives. Do you know someone who is still playing the blaming game? It's a game you can't win - ever.

End Times, Part One

God's Minute

> But there were also false prophets among the people, just as there will be false teachers among you. They will secretly introduce destructive heresies, even denying the sovereign Lord who bought them—bringing swift destruction on themselves. Many will follow their shameful ways and will bring the way of truth into disrepute. In their greed these teachers will exploit you with stories they have made up. Their condemnation has long been hanging over them, and their destruction has not been sleeping.
>
> —2 Peter 2:1-3 (NIV)

The Pastor's Minute

Do you believe that we are now living in the end times?

I want to share with you some of the biblical signs of what the Bible calls "the last days" - the days just before Jesus comes back for His Church.

The Pastor's Minute

In Second Timothy, Saint Paul said that in the last days, perilous times would come. The word "perilous" means "high risk." In other words, one of the characteristics of the last days would be danger, many hidden traps even though everything may look great. It will be a time of political high risk. You'll have to watch every word you say for fear of offending someone.

High risk socially. I was stunned to read in the Arizona Republic newspaper that one man with AIDS knowingly infected over 100 women. High Risk.

It'd be a high risk time religiously as well. Today there are over 2,000 offbeat cults which claim collectively over 10 million members. It amazes me to hear people criticizing good churches but never saying anything about these cults.

Anyway, continue to watch for high-risk days - and you'll know Christ's return is near.

End Times, Part Two

God's Minute

> Likewise every good tree bears good fruit, but a bad tree bears bad fruit. A good tree cannot bear bad fruit, and a bad tree cannot bear good fruit. Every tree that does not bear good fruit is cut down and thrown into the fire. Thus, by their fruit you will recognize them.
>
> —Matthew 7:17-20 (NIV)

The Pastor's Minute

We are looking at world conditions in what the Bible calls the last days. Saint Paul said the last days would be marked as high risk, dangerous times.

Jesus gave us another indicator - a sign - when He said it would be a time of much deception. There would be political, social, and religious deceivers. Only those who carefully read their Bibles will know the difference between the true and the false.

Jesus likened deceivers to a brood of vipers - snakes. I saw a green mamba at the Oklahoma Zoo some time ago. It's a little snake, and it's color is an appealing beautiful green. It looks like it could be a friendly pet. Yet, one bite from the East African Green Mamba snake and you'll have less than 30 minutes to live because of its deadly toxins. I thought about what Jesus had said about deceivers when I saw that snake.

They look great, but they carry a deadly toxin. The vaccine for deception is to regularly read your Bible, pray daily, and find a good Bible-believing church to get involved in.

End Times, Part Three

God's Minute

> There will be great earthquakes, famines and pestilences in various places, and fearful events and great signs from heaven.
>
> —Luke 21:11 (NIV)

> Nation will rise against nation, and kingdom against kingdom. There will be famines and earthquakes in various places.
>
> —Matthew 24:7 (NIV)

The Pastor's Minute

Are we now living at the climax of the ages? We've been looking at the biblical "last days" and signs that point to the last days.

Saint Paul said the last days would be marked by danger. Jesus said there would be massive deception in those days. He also said there would be an increase in the frequency of earthquakes.

Dr. Carl Baugh, a scientist and archeologist, recently reported that the internal temperature of the earth is supposed to be about 6,000 degrees. Yet geophysicists are now measuring (for some reason) temperatures in excess of 12,000 degrees. Now, that's more heat than there is on the sun's surface. He went on to say that it appears that there is strange thermonuclear activity going on in the center of the earth right now.

He claims that's the reason we've seen such a rise in earthquakes in this past decade.

Interesting, isn't it? Could Jesus have been predicting the day in which we now live? It's hard to say, but I think it may be more than a weird coincidence.

End Times, Part Four

God's Minute

> But Daniel, keep this prophecy a secret; seal it up so that it will not be understood until the end times, when travel and education shall be vastly increased!
>
> —Daniel 12:4 (TLB)

The Pastor's Minute

Will Jesus really come back for His church just prior to the world's greatest hour of sorrow? We've been taking a hard look at biblical signs of the times.

The prophet Daniel was given two indicators which would signal the "last days." First, the angel told him that human travel would vastly increase. Interestingly, today U.S. citizens alone spend 32.9 billion dollars each year on travel alone. In 1947, only 7 million people traveled by air. In 1997, 550 million people traveled by air.

The second sign was amazing. Knowledge would increase. The Hebrew words may read something like this: "It will be a time known as the Information Age." Wow! Today, every 60 seconds, an estimated 2,000 single spaced typewritten pages are being added to man's knowledge storehouse. That's every minute. And I believe this day is called the "Information Age."

Now, I may be wrong, but if I am, it sure is a phenomenal coincidence that the Bible is so accurate in its pinpoint predictions concerning these so-called "last days." Read about it yourself and see if you agree with me.

Why I Don't Wash

God's Minute

> Purge me with hyssop, and I shall be clean: wash me, and I shall be whiter than snow.
>
> —Psalm 51:7

> Create in me a clean heart, O God; and renew a right spirit within me.
>
> —Psalm 51:10

The Pastor's Minute

We all need to wash our bodies daily, and we know it. There's no argument!

Someone has made a list of excuses for not washing. Maybe you're familiar with some of them.

1. I was made to wash as a child.

2. People who wash are hypocrites - they reckon they're cleaner than other people.

3. There are so many different kinds of soap, I can never decide which one is right.

4. I used to wash, but it got boring so I stopped.

5. I still wash on special occasions like Christmas or Easter.

6. None of my friends wash.

7. I'm still young. When I'm older and have got a bit dirtier, I might start washing.

8. I really don't have time.

9. The bathroom's never warm enough.

10. People who make soap are only after your money.

Yes, there are perhaps endless reasons why a person shouldn't be forced to wash each day; just like there are endless reasons why a person shouldn't have to attend church. But church is where we learn about how to have a personal relationship with Jesus. He is the One who does for us what soap and water can never do — make us clean on the inside.

Are you attending a good church? Or are you inventing reasons why the Lord doesn't deserve your time? Only you can answer that question.

Old Fifth-A-Day

God's Minute

> A man with leprosy came and knelt before him and said, "Lord, if you are willing, you can make me clean." Jesus reached out his hand and touched the man. "I am willing," he said. "Be clean!" Immediately he was cured of his leprosy.
>
> —Matthew 8:2-3 (NIV)

> And Jesus said unto him, This day is salvation come to this house, forsomuch as he also is a son of Abraham. For the Son of man is come to seek and to save that which was lost.
>
> —Luke 19:9-10

The Pastor's Minute

Roy was an abusive, addicted man. Mean, selfish, and abusive to those who loved him, he continued drinking a fifth of whiskey every day. It earned him the title of "Old Fifth-A-Day."

Somehow, someone invited Roy to attend Mount Hope Church, and surprisingly he came. He heard things he had never heard before. Things like: God loves you and has the power to give you a new start in life. You see, others believed Roy was hopeless.

Well, when I gave the invitation for people to come and personally meet the Savior, Old Fifth-A-Day, Roy, stumbled up to that old-fashioned altar and prayed a simple prayer. In an instant, a miracle happened. A divine deliverance took place.

Roy got his sins forgiven, got a new start in life, and hasn't touched a drop of liquor since. Not only that, he hasn't even had the desire to pick up his old smoking habit. That was twelve years ago, and Roy is still enjoying and rejoicing in his miracle of an alcohol free life.

Do you have a habit that needs to be broken from your life? God is waiting to take that habit away from you. All you have to do is ask.

Jezebel

God's Minute

> But God commendeth his love toward us, in that, while we were yet sinners, Christ died for us.

> — Romans 5:8

> Come, let's talk this over! says the Lord; no matter how deep the stain of your sins, I can take it out and make you as clean as freshly fallen snow. Even if you are stained as red as crimson, I can make you white as wool.

> —Isaiah 1:18 (TLB)

The Pastor's Minute

After twenty years in full-time Gospel ministry, I've collected a series of pretty interesting and amazing stories. Like the time I was giving a Gospel invitation, sort of like Billy Graham does in his crusades, inviting people to come forward to be forgiven and get a new life from God.

I couldn't believe my eyes. Coming down the aisle was a lady in a mini skirt and five inch spiked high heals and more makeup than a barn has paint. I thought, surely, Jezebel had come back to life. Well, she prayed with us, we gave her a Bible and a New Life book, and that was that. Frankly, I wondered if anything really happened.

The next week on Sunday morning, she was back in church. Only, now she looked radiant; she just glowed. She brought two friends up for prayer after the service. Turns out she had been a practicing prostitute but now wanted to be a woman of God.

Did it work? That was eleven years ago, and today Lisa is happily married and has a lovely family. God gave her a new life.

How about you? Do you need a new start in life? Well, God is still in the business of making new beginnings for those who ask. It really is simple. Do it today. You'll be glad you did.

Kim

God's Minute

> And he arose out of the synagogue, and entered into Simon's house. And Simon's wife's mother was taken with a great fever; and they besought him for her. And he stood over her, and rebuked the fever; and it left her: and immediately she arose and ministered unto them. Now when the sun was setting, all they that had any sick with divers diseases brought them unto him; and he laid his hands on every one of them, and healed them.
>
> —Luke 4:38-40

The Pastor's Minute

Just a month or so ago, during a routine examination, Kim discovered that she had a lump in her breast. The doctor was quite concerned, ordered a mammogram and, subsequently, other even more accurate medical tests.

You can imagine Kim's despair — barely in her forties, a mother of two beautiful children, and the wife of an associate minister here at Mount Hope Church. Now she would soon be submitting to a biopsy that could lead to the dreaded procedure: every woman's nightmare.

Before the scheduled biopsy, Kim's husband asked several of his friends from Mount Hope to begin to pray. And we did pray. Well, Kim went in for the biopsy and created quite a stir at the hospital. The surgeons could find no lump at all. It was on the x-rays, but when they went in, it was gone — disappeared. I think you can appreciate Kim's excitement and gratitude to God.

Have you been given a bad report from the doctor? Have you been ill and are needing the Great Physician? He is only a prayer away.

Eternal Life

God's Minute

Whereas ye know what shall be on the morrow. For what is your life? It is even a vapour, that appeareth for a little time, and then vanisheth away.

—James 4:14

Give thanks unto the Father, which hath made us meet to be partakers of the inheritance of the saints in light: Who hath delivered us from the power of darkness, and hath translated us into the kingdom of his dear Son.

—Colossians 1:12-14

The Pastor's Minute

Nineteen years ago, I witnessed a man callously throw a small kitten out of his car as he sped by the front of my house.

The little buff-colored kitten limped up to my door and began to purr. She seemed afraid, lonely, hurt, and hungry. So I fed her some tuna fish and prepared her a dish of milk, and she decided she would stay.

For nineteen years, Bobo was my loyal friend. The other night, my little friend died in my arms. She was 13 in cat years.

It's hard to lose a pet. It's even harder to lose a human loved one. But it eases the pain to know that life goes on beyond this one - and when we know our loved one has made peace with God, it brings great comfort.

Jesus promises eternal life for those who will follow Him.

I don't know if cats go to Heaven or not - I hope so. I want to see Bobo again. And even better than that, I want to see you in Heaven someday too!

A New Start

God's Minute

> And when you draw close to God, God will draw close to you.
>
> —James 5:8 (TLB)

> Come to me, all ye that labour and are heavy laden, and I will give you rest.
>
> —Matthew 11:28

The Pastor's Minute

Dear Friend, Have you ever wished you could start your life all over again? If so, I have good news for you.

Jesus, God's Son, made a way for you to experience a brand new life. Yes, you can start over regardless of how many wrongs you've done or how "messed up" you may feel right now.

Jesus died on the cross 2000 years ago so that men and women, boys and girls of all ages may be forgiven. Right now, at this very moment, JESUS forgives you all of the wrong you've ever done. But in order to experience that forgiveness and receive a brand new life, you must accept Christ as your Savior. He is mankind's only hope. We can't save ourselves from the guilt, pain, and consequences of sin. So Jesus did it for us.

Nobody can be fit for Heaven apart from accepting Christ not even the most moral and religious person in the world. Jesus Himself said that nobody will ever get to God unless he comes through Jesus. He said:

> "I am the way, the truth, and the life: No man cometh unto the Father, but by me." —John 14:6

and Saint Paul put it this way:

> "For there is one God, and one mediator between God and men, the man Christ Jesus." —1 Timothy 2:5

And so it's true! There's only one way to experience forgiveness and receive a new start in life. It's through the Lord Jesus Christ! And wow! He is waiting to work miracles in your life because He loves you no matter what condition you're in right now. He doesn't say, "Clean up your act, and I'll accept you!" Instead, He says, "Come to me now just the way you are, and I'll give you a new life!"

No Strings Attached

God's Minute

> Therefore if any man be in Christ, he is a new creature: Old things are passed away; behold, all things become new.
>
> —2 Corinthians 5:17

Pastor's Minute

Can you believe it? No strings attached. God's forgiveness, acceptance, and power are available to you right now just for the asking.

God has done His part to give you a new life here on earth and some day a home in Heaven. Now it's up to you.

Come to Jesus as you are (Romans 3:23).

Admit your helplessness to save yourself (Romans 6:23, Luke 18:13).

Ask Jesus to be your Savior and to give you a new start (2 Corinthians 5:17).

Confess with your mouth that He is Lord (Romans 10:9).

By faith receive Christ into your life (John 1: 11, 12).

The burden of sin will be quickly rolled away if you do these things. God is standing by you right now to hear you pray. He's ready to send Jesus into your life and is calling the angels together for a celebration in Heaven - a celebration over YOU!

> ...joy shall be in heaven over one sinner that repenteth, more than over ninety and nine just persons, which need no repentance.
>
> —Luke 15:7

Why not pray this prayer? It will help lead you to a brand new life. It's what I call a simple prayer of salvation:

Dear God,

I come to you in the Name of Jesus. Your Word says in John 6:37 that if I turn to You, You will in no way cast me out, but You will take me in, just as I am. I thank You, God, for that.

You also said in Romans 10:13 that if I call upon You, I'll be saved. I'm calling on You, Lord, so I know You have now saved me.

I believe Jesus died on the cross for me, and that He was raised from the dead. I now confess Him as my Lord.

I now have a new life. My sins are gone, and I have a new start, beginning NOW!

Thank You, Lord! Amen

About The Author

Dave Williams is pastor of Mount Hope Church and International Outreach Ministries, with world headquarters in Lansing, Michigan. He has served for over 20 years, leading the church in Lansing from 226 to over 4000 today. Dave sends trained ministers into unreached cities to establish disciple-making churches, and, as a result, today has "branch" churches in the United States, Philippines, and in Africa.

Dave is the founder and president of Mount Hope Bible Training Institute, a fully accredited institute for training ministers and lay people for the work of the ministry. He has authored 45 books including the fifteen-time best seller, *The Start of Something Wonderful* (with over 2,000,000 books sold), and more recently, *The Miracle Results of Fasting*, and *The Road To Radical Riches*.

The Pacesetter's Path telecast is Dave's weekly television program seen over a syndicated network of secular stations, and nationally over the Sky Angel satellite system. Dave has produced over 125 audio cassette programs including the nationally acclaimed School of Pacesetting Leadership which is being used as a training program in churches around the United States, and in Bible Schools in South Africa and the Philippines. He is a popular speaker at conferences, seminars, and conventions. His speaking ministry has taken him across America, Africa, Europe, Asia, and other parts of the world.

Along with his wife, Mary Jo, Dave established The Dave and Mary Jo Williams Charitable Mission (Strategic Global Mission), a mission's ministry for providing scholarships to pioneer pastors and grants to inner-city children's ministries.

Dave's articles and reviews have appeared in national magazines such as Advance, The Pentecostal Evangel, Ministries Today, The Lansing Magazine, The Detroit Free Press and others. Dave, as a private pilot, flies for fun. He is married, has two grown children, and lives in Delta Township, Michigan.

You may write to Pastor Dave Williams:

P.O. Box 80825

Lansing, MI 48908-0825

Please include your special prayer requests when you write, or you may call the Mount Hope Global Prayer Center anytime: (517) 327-PRAY

DECAPOLIS
PUBLISHING

For a catalog of products, call:

1-517-321-2780 or

1-800-888-7284

or visit us on the web at:

www.mounthopechurch.org

For Your Spiritual Growth

Here's the help you need for your spiritual journey. These books will encourage you, and give you guidance as you seek to draw close to Jesus and learn of Him. Prepare yourself for fantastic growth!

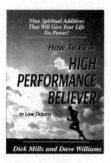

HOW TO BE A HIGH PERFORMANCE BELIEVER
Pour in the nine spiritual additives for real power in your Christian life.

SECRET OF POWER WITH GOD
Tap into the real power with God; the power of prayer. It will change your life!

THE NEW LIFE...
You can get off to a great start on your exciting life with Jesus! Prepare for something wonderful.

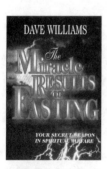

MIRACLE RESULTS OF FASTING
You can receive MIRACLE benefits, spiritually and physically, with this practical Christian discipline.

WHAT TO DO IF YOU MISS THE RAPTURE
If you miss the Rapture, there may still be hope, but you need to follow these clear survival tactics.

THE AIDS PLAGUE
Is there hope? Yes, but only Jesus can bring a total and lasting cure to AIDS.

These and other books available from Dave Williams and:

DECAPOLIS PUBLISHING

For Your Spiritual Growth

Here's the help you need for your spiritual journey. These books will encourage you, and give you guidance as you seek to draw close to Jesus and learn of Him. Prepare yourself for fantastic growth!

THE ART OF PACESETTING LEADERSHIP
You can become a successful leader with this proven leadership development course.

GIFTS THAT SHAPE YOUR LIFE
Learn which ministry best fits you, and discover your God-given personality gifts, as well as the gifts of others.

GROWING UP IN OUR FATHER'S FAMILY
You can have a family relationship with your heavenly father. Learn how God cares for you.

SUPERNATURAL SOULWINNING
How will we reach our family, friends, and neighbors in this short time before Christ's return?

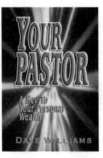

YOUR PASTOR: A KEY TO YOUR PERSONAL WEALTH
By honoring your pastor you can actually be setting yourself up for a financial blessing from God!

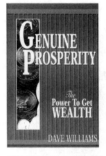

GENUINE PROSPERITY
Learn what it means to be truly prosperous! God gives us the power to get wealth!

These and other books available from Dave Williams and:

DECAPOLIS PUBLISHING

For Your Spiritual Growth

Here's the help you need for your spiritual jour-ney. These books will encourage you, and give you guidance as you seek to draw close to Jesus and learn of Him. Prepare yourself for fantastic growth!

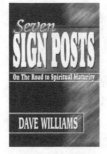

SOMEBODY OUT THERE NEEDS YOU
Along with the gift of salvation comes the great privilege of spreading the gospel of Jesus Christ.

SEVEN SIGNPOSTS TO SPIRITUAL MATURITY
Examine your life to see where you are on the road to spiritual maturity.

THE PASTORS PAY
How much is your pastor worth? Who should set his pay? Discover the scriptural guidelines for paying your pastor.

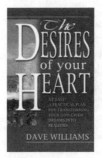

DECEPTION, DELUSION & DESTRUCTION
Recognize spiritual deception and unmask spiritual blindness.

THE ROAD TO RADICAL RICHES
Are you ready to jump from "barely getting by" to Gods plan for putting you on the road to Radical Riches?

THE DESIRES OF YOUR HEART
Yes, Jesus wants to give you the desires of your heart, and make them realities.

These and other books available from Dave Williams and:

DECAPOLIS
PUBLISHING

For Your Successful Life

These video cassettes will give you successful principles to apply to your whole life. Each a different topic, and each a fantastic teaching of how living by God's Word can give you total success!

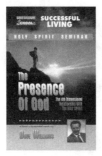

THE PRESENCE OF GOD
Find out how you can have a more dynamic relationship with the Holy Spirit.

FILLED WITH THE HOLY SPIRIT
You can rejoice and share with others in this wonderful experience of God.

GIFTS THAT CHANGE YOUR WORLD
Learn which ministry best fits you, and discover your God-given personality gifts, as well as the gifts of others.

THE SCHOOL OF PACESETTING LEADERSHIP
Leaders are made, not born. You can become a successful leader with this proven leadership development course.

MIRACLE RESULTS OF FASTING
Fasting is your secret weapon in spiritual warfare. Learn how you'll benefit spiritually and physically! Six video messages.

A SPECIAL LADY
If you feel used and abused, this video will show you how you really are in the eyes of Jesus. You are special!

These and other videos available from Dave Williams and:

DECAPOLIS
PUBLISHING

For Your Successful Life

These video cassettes will give you successful principles to apply to your whole life. Each a different topic, and each a fantastic teaching of how living by God's Word can give you total success!

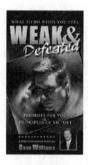

HOW TO BE A HIGH PERFORMANCE BELIEVER
Pour in the nine spiritual additives for real power in your Christian life.

THE UGLY WORMS OF JUDGMENT
Recognizing the decay of judgment in your life is your first step back into God's fullness.

WHAT TO DO WHEN YOU FEEL WEAK AND DEFEATED
Learn about God's plan to bring you out of defeat and into His principles of victory!

WHY SOME ARE NOT HEALED
Discover the obstacles that hold people back from receiving their miracle and how God can help them receive the very best!

BREAKING THE POWER OF POVERTY
The principality of mammon will try to keep you in poverty. Put God FIRST and watch Him bring you into a wealthy place.

HERBS FOR HEALTH
A look at the concerns and fears of modern medicine. Learn the correct ways to open the doors to your healing.

These and other videos available from Dave Williams and:

DECAPOLIS PUBLISHING

Running Your Race

These simple but powerful audio cassette singles will help give you the edge you need. Run your race to win!

LONELY IN THE MIDST OF A CROWD
Loneliness is a devastating disease. Learn how to trust and count on others to help.

HERBS FOR HEALTH
A look at the concerns and fears of modern medicine. Learn the correct ways to open the doors to your healing.

HOW TO GET ANYTHING YOU WANT
You can learn the way to get anything you want from God!

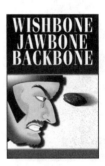

WISHBONE, JAWBONE, BACKBONE
Learn about King David, and how his three "bones" for success can help you in your life quest.

FATAL ENTICEMENTS
Learn how you can avoid the vice-like grip of sin and it's fatal enticements that hold people captive.

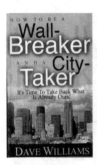

HOW TO BE A WALL BREAKER AND A CITY TAKER
You can be a powerful force for advancing the Kingdom of Jesus Christ!

These and other audio tapes available from Dave Williams and:

DECAPOLIS PUBLISHING

Expanding Your Faith

These exciting audio teaching series will help
you to grow and mature in your walk with Christ.
Get ready for amazing new adventures in faith!

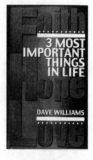

WHY DO SOME SUFFER
Find out why some people
seem to have suffering in
their lives, and find out
how to avoid it in your life.

SIN'S GRIP
Learn how you can avoid
the vice-like grip of sin and
it's fatal enticements that
hold people captive.

FAITH, HOPE, & LOVE
Listen and let these three
"most important things in
life" change you.

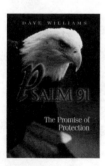

PSALM 91
THE PROMISE OF
PROTECTION
Everyone is looking for
protection in these perilous
times. God promises
protection for those who
rest in Him.

DEVELOPING
THE SPIRIT OF A
CONQUEROR
You can be a conqueror
through Christ! Also, find
out how to *keep* those
things that you have
conquered.

YOUR SPECTACULAR
MIND
Identify wrong thinking
and negative influences in
your life.

**These and other audio tapes
available from Dave Williams and:**

DECAPOLIS
PUBLISHING

Expanding Your Faith

These exciting audio teaching series will help you to grow and mature in your walk with Christ. Get ready for amazing new adventures in faith!

ABCs OF SUCCESS AND HAPPINESS
Learn how to go after God's promises for your life. Happiness and success can be yours today!

FORGIVENESS
The miracle remedy for many of life's problems is found in this basic key for living.

UNTANGLING YOUR TROUBLES
You can be a "trouble untangler" with the help of Jesus!

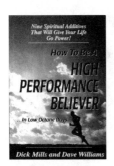

HOW TO BE A HIGH PERFORMANCE BELIEVER
Put in the nine spiritual additives to help run your race and get the prize!

BEING A DISCIPLE AND MAKING DISCIPLES
You can learn to be a "disciple maker" to almost anyone.

HOW TO HELP YOUR PASTOR & CHURCH SUCCEED
You can be an integral part of your church's & pastor's success.

These and other audio tapes available from Dave Williams and:

DECAPOLIS PUBLISHING

More Products by Dave Williams

BOOK Title	Price
The New Life — The Start Of Something Wonderful	$1.95
End Times Bible Prophecy	$4.95
Seven Sign Posts On the Road To Spiritual Maturity	$4.95
Somebody Out There Needs You	$4.95
Growing Up In Our Father's Family	$4.95
Grief & Mourning	$7.95
The World Beyond — Mysteries Of Heaven	$7.95
The Secret Of Power With God	$7.95
What To Do If You Miss the Rapture	$9.95
Genuine Prosperity	$9.95
The Miracle Results Of Fasting	$9.95
How To Be A High Performance Believer	$9.95
Gifts That Shape Your Life & Change Your World	$10.95
Road To Radical Riches	$19.95

CD Title	Num. of CDs	Price
Middle East Crisis	1	$12.00
Setting Our Houses In Order	1	$12.00
Too Much Baggage?	1	$12.00
Jesus Loves Sinners	1	$12.00
How To Get Your Breakthrough	1	$12.00
Amazing Power Of Desire	1	$12.00
Wounded Spirit	1	$12.00
The Attack On America (Sept. 11, 2001)	1	$12.00
Radical Wealth	5	$60.00

VIDEO Title	Num. of Videos	Price
What To Do When You Are Going Through Hell	1	$19.95
Acres Of Diamonds — The Valley Of Baca	1	$19.95
120 Elite Warriors	1	$19.95
What To Do If You Miss the Rapture	1	$19.95
Regaining Your Spiritual Momentum	1	$19.95
Herbs For Health	1	$19.95
TheDestructive Power Of Legalism	1	$19.95
4 Ugly Worms Of Judgment	1	$19.95
Grief and Mourning	1	$19.95
Breaking the Power Of Poverty	1	$19.95
Triple Benefits Of Fasting	1	$19.95
Why Some Are Not Healed	2	$39.95
Miracle Results Of Fasting	3	$59.95
ABCs Of Success and Happiness	3	$59.95
Gifts That Shape Your Life and Change Your World	5	$99.95

AUDIO Title	Num. of Tapes	Price
Lonely In the Midst Of a Crowd	1	$6.00
How To Get Anything You Want	1	$6.00
Untangling Your Troubles	2	$12.00
Healing Principles In the Ministry Of Jesus	2	$12.00
Acres Of Diamonds — The Valley Of Baca	2	$12.00
Finding Peace	2	$12.00
Criticize & Judge	2	$12.00
Judgment On America	2	$12.00
Triple Benefits Of Fasting	2	$12.00
Global Confusion	2	$12.00
The Cure For a Broken Heart	2	$12.00
Help! I'm Getting Older	2	$12.00
Regaining Your Spiritual Momentum	2	$12.00
The Destructive Power Of Legalism	2	$12.00
Three Most Important Things In Life	3	$18.00
The Final Series	3	$18.00
The Mysteries of Heaven	3	$18.00
Dave Williams' Crash Course In Intercessory Prayer	3	$18.00
Forgiveness — The Miracle Remedy	4	$24.00
How Long Until the End	4	$24.00
What To Do When You Feel Weak and Defeated	4	$24.00
Sin's Grip	4	$24.00
Why Some Are Not Healed	4	$24.00
Bible Cures	4	$24.00
Belial	4	$24.00
God is Closer Than You Think	5	$30.00
Decoding the Apocalypse	5	$30.00
Winning Your Inner Conflict	5	$30.00
Radical Wealth	5	$30.00
Violent Action For Your Wealth	5	$30.00
The Presence Of God	6	$36.00
Your Spectacular Mind	6	$36.00
The Miracle Results of Fasting	6	$36.00
Developing the Spirit Of a Conqueror	6	$36.00
Why Do Some Suffer	6	$36.00
Overcoming Life's Adversities	6	$36.00
Faith Steps	6	$36.00
ABCs For Success & Happiness	6	$36.00
The Best Of Dave Williams	6	$36.00
How To Help Your Pastor & Church Succeed	8	$48.00
Being a Disciple & Making Disciples	8	$48.00
High Performance Believer	8	$48.00
True Or False	8	$48.00
The End Times	8	$48.00
The Beatitudes — Success 101	8	$48.00
Hearing the Voice Of God	10	$60.00
Gifts That Shape Your Life — Personality Gifts	10	$60.00
Gifts That Shape Your Life & Change Your World — Ministry Gifts	10	$60.00
Daniel Parts 1 & 2 (Both parts 6 tapes each)	12	$72.00
Roadblocks To Your Radical Wealth	12	$72.00
Revelation Parts 1 & 2 (part 1 - 6 tapes; part 2 - 8 tapes)	14	$84.00

Mount Hope Ministries

Mount Hope Missions & International Outreach
Care Ministries, Deaf Ministries
& Support Groups
Access to Christ for the Physically Impaired
Community Outreach Ministries
Mount Hope Youth Ministries
Mount Hope Bible Training Institute
The Hope Store and Decapolis Publishing
The Pacesetter's Path Telecast
The Pastor's Minute Radio Broadcast
Mount Hope Children's Ministry
Champions Club and Sidewalk Sunday School
The Saturday Care Clinic

When you're facing a struggle and need someone
to pray with you, please call us at (517) 321-CARE
or (517) 327-PRAY. We have pastors on duty 24
hours a day. We know you hurt sometimes and
need a pastor, a minister, or a prayer partner. There
will be ministers and prayer partners here for you.

If you'd like to write, we'd be honored to pray for
you. Our address is:

MOUNT HOPE CHURCH
202 S. CREYTS RD.
LANSING, MI 48917
(517) 321-CARE or (517) 321-2780
FAX (517)321-6332
TDD (517) 321-8200

www.mounthopechurch.org

email: mhc@mounthopechurch.org

West of the Lansing Mall, on Creyts at Michigan Ave.

What people are saying about

The New Life ... The Start of Something Wonderful

"The material is excellent and will be used for the glory of God!" Dr. David Yonggi Cho, Full Gospel Central Church, **Seoul, KOREA**

"We are in need of more books, *THE NEW LIFE*. This class has met with great enthusiasm. The study is doing a real good ministry. Thank you." **Pastor GM, Warsaw, IN**

"I am very excited about your book, *THE NEW LIFE ... THE START OF SOMETHING WONDERFUL*. It has been most helpful and I would like to purchase more." **JA, Camilla, GA**

"Please send me 100 books (*THE NEW LIFE*). We received one from our pastor and like them so much that we want to give them to new Christians in the jail." **PC, Muskegon, MI**

"I read your book, *THE NEW LIFE ... THE START OF SOMETHING WONDERFUL*, and I was very impressed with its simplicity and its complete guideline to spiritual growth. I would recommend it to every believer, old or new." **AF, Church Hill, TN**

"Praise the Lord for your study booklet, *THE NEW LIFE ... THE START OF SOMETHING WONDERFUL*! We use it regularly for new Christians." **BT, Yorkville, IL**

Dave Williams

English & Spanish Versions Available

SPECIAL OFFER

One Case (150 books) $142.50 + Shipping

Offer expires December 31, 2005

ORDER YOUR COPY TODAY!

How to begin a regular prayer life

How to overcome temptation

How to read and study the Bible

How to share Christ with others

How to select the right associates

THE HOPE STORE • 202 S. Creyts Road • Lansing, MI 48917
TOLL FREE 1-800-888-7284